W9-AMB-256

Assessment Sourcebook

Includes multiple choice, constructed response, and writing-in-math items

Grade 1

- Placement Test
- Quick Check Masters
- Topic Tests
- Benchmark Tests
- End-of-Year Test
- Basic-Facts Timed Tests

Scott Foresman·Addison Wesley

enVisionMATH®
Common Core

PEARSON

Glenview, Illinois • Boston Massachusetts • Chandler, Arizona • Upper Saddle River, New Jersey

ISBN-13: 978-0-328-73132-9

ISBN-10: 0-328-73132-3

2 3 4 5 6 7 8 9 10 V016 19 18 17 16 15 14 13 12

Contents

Placement Test

Quick Check Masters
Topics 1–16

Topic Tests
Topics 1–16

Benchmark Tests
Topics 1–4
Topics 5–8
Topics 9–12
Topics 13–16

End-of-Year Test

Basic-Facts Timed Tests

Name _____

1.

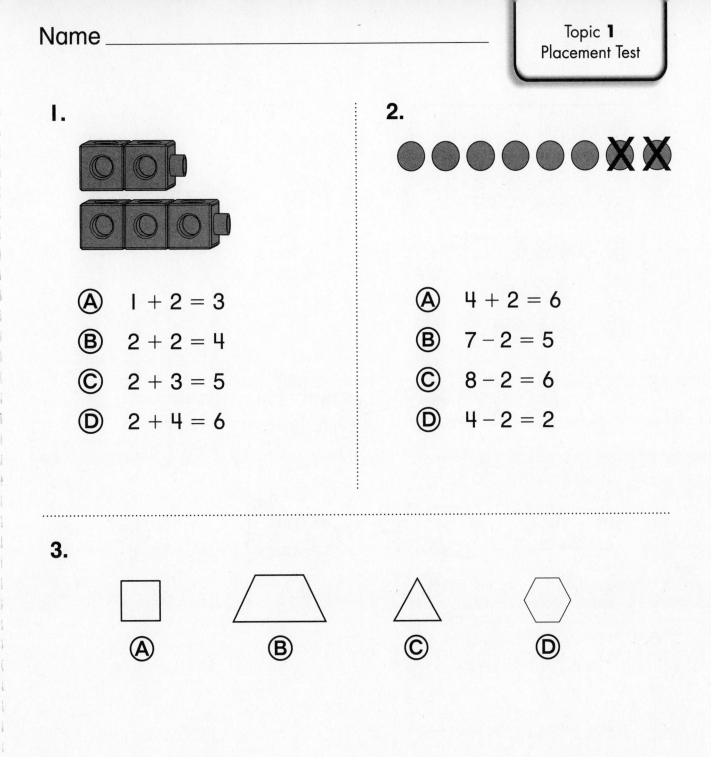

Ⓐ $1 + 2 = 3$

Ⓑ $2 + 2 = 4$

Ⓒ $2 + 3 = 5$

Ⓓ $2 + 4 = 6$

2.

Ⓐ $4 + 2 = 6$

Ⓑ $7 - 2 = 5$

Ⓒ $8 - 2 = 6$

Ⓓ $4 - 2 = 2$

3.

Ⓐ   Ⓑ   Ⓒ   Ⓓ

Directions Have children mark the best answer. **1.** Which addition sentence shows joining of the cubes? **2.** Which subtraction sentence shows how many counters are left? **3.** Which object is a hexagon?

Name _____

4.

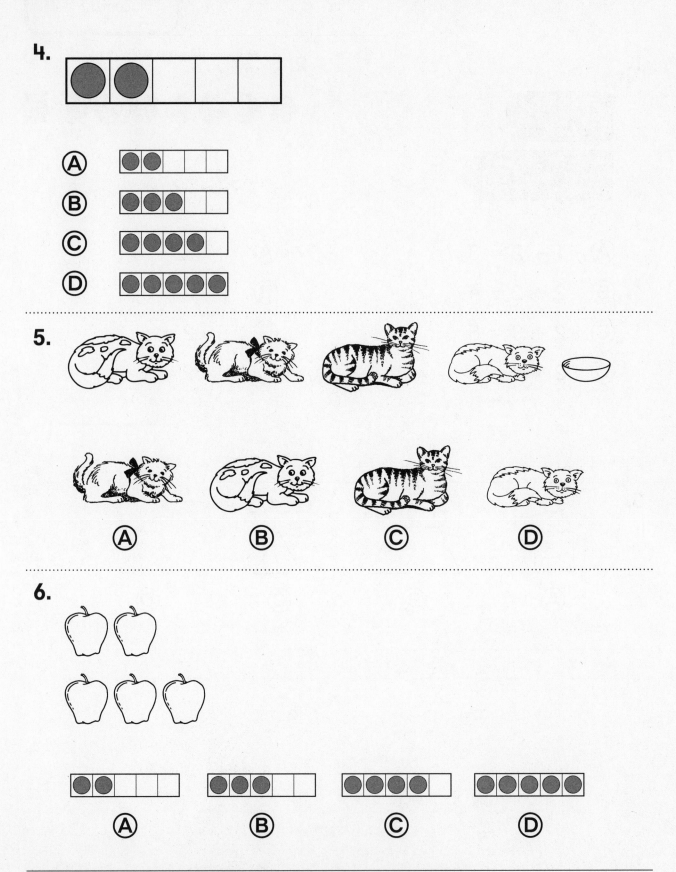

A

B

C

D

5.

Ⓐ Ⓑ Ⓒ Ⓓ

6.

Ⓐ Ⓑ Ⓒ Ⓓ

Directions Have children mark the best answer. **4.** Which shows 1 counter greater than the group shown? **5.** Which cat is third in line for water? **6.** Which shows 5?

Name _____

7.

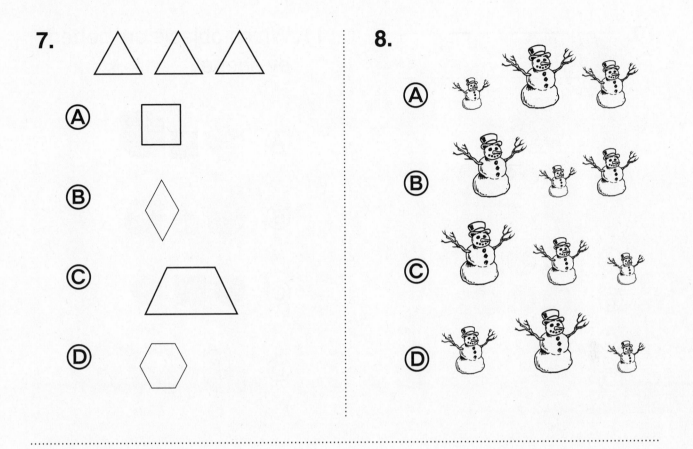

Ⓐ ☐

Ⓑ ◇

Ⓒ ⬯

Ⓓ ⬡

8.

Ⓐ

Ⓑ

Ⓒ

Ⓓ

9.

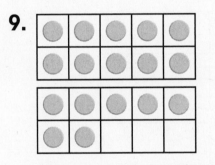

Ⓐ ten and 8 ones

Ⓑ ten and 7 ones

Ⓒ ten and 3 ones

Ⓓ ten and 5 ones

Directions Have children mark the best answer. **7.** Which shows a shape that can be made from three triangles?
8. Which shows the snowmen in order from tallest to shortest? **9.** How many tens and ones does this show?

Name _____

10.

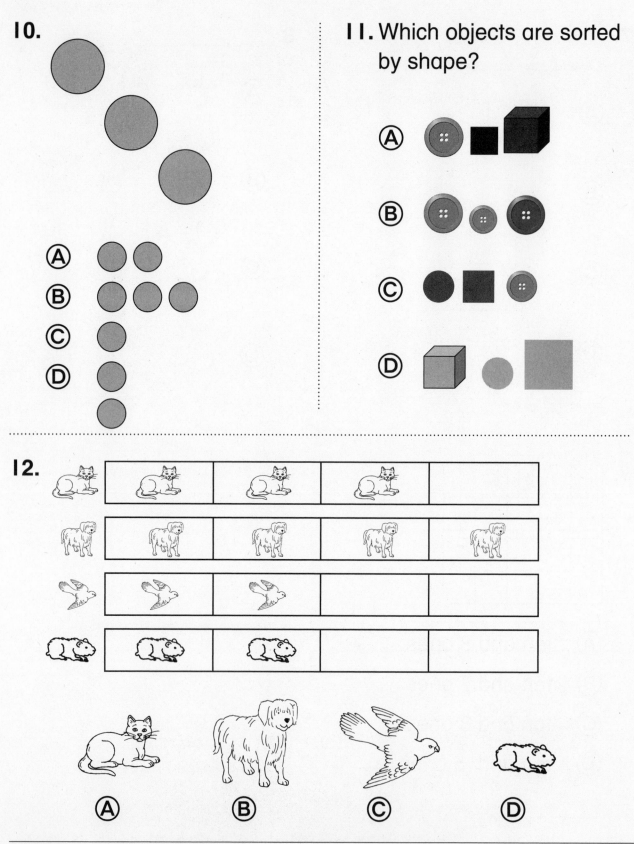

11. Which objects are sorted by shape?

Ⓐ

Ⓑ

Ⓒ

Ⓓ

12.

Ⓐ   Ⓑ   Ⓒ   Ⓓ

Directions Have children mark the best answer. **10.** Which shows the counters arranged in a different way?
11. How are the objects in the group sorted? **12.** Which pet is there the most of on the graph?

Name _____

1. Marnie has 5 hair ribbons.
Her sister gives her 5 more.
How many ribbons does
Marnie have now?

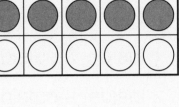

    (A) 5

    (B) 8

    (C) 9

    (D) 10

2. Which number tells how many?

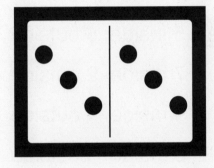

    (A) 10

    (B) 8

    (C) 6

    (D) 4

3. Complete the picture to solve.
Write the number.

Kim reads 6 pages.
Then she reads 3 more.
Tell the number of pages
Kim reads in all.

_____

- - - - - - - - -

_____ pages

Name _____

1. Which tells about the
flowers in the picture?

Ⓐ　1 inside　3 outside　4 in all

Ⓑ　2 inside　4 outside　6 in all

Ⓒ　1 inside　5 outside　6 in all

Ⓓ　4 inside　4 outside　8 in all

2. Which shows a different way
to group the birds?

Ⓐ　5 inside　5 outside　10 in all

Ⓑ　7 inside　2 outside　9 in all

Ⓒ　4 inside　4 outside　8 in all

Ⓓ　3 inside　4 outside　7 in all

3. Draw a picture to solve.

Tito has 6 white mice.
Some mice are inside the cage.
Some mice are outside the cage.

_____ _____ _____
　inside　　outside　　in all

Name _____

1. Which shows the missing part of 8?

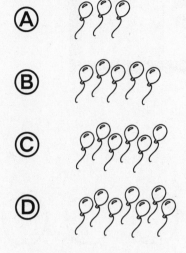 and _____

Ⓐ ✦✦✦

Ⓑ ✦✦✦✦

Ⓒ ✦✦✦✦

Ⓓ ✦✦✦✦✦

2. Katy has 8 beads.
One part is 5.
Which is the other part?

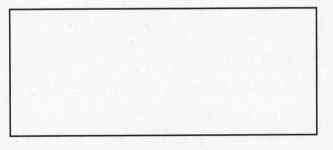

Ⓐ 13

Ⓑ 5

Ⓒ 4

Ⓓ 3

3. Writing in Math
Draw a picture to solve.
Write numbers to tell about the parts of the whole.

Max sees 8 flowers.
Some flowers are red.
The rest are yellow.

_____ and _____ is 8.

1. Which part of 9
is the picture missing?

Ⓐ 3

Ⓑ 2

Ⓒ 1

Ⓓ 0

2. Dan has 4 apples.
How many more does he
need to make 9 apples?

Ⓐ   5 apples

Ⓑ   6 apples

Ⓒ   7 apples

Ⓓ   8 apples

3. Draw a picture to solve.
Use numbers to tell about
the parts of the whole.

There are 9 kittens at the
pet store.
Some kittens are white and
the rest are black.

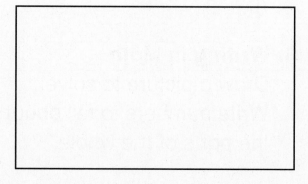

_____ and _____ is 9.

Q1·4

Name _____

1. Which one matches the parts in the picture?

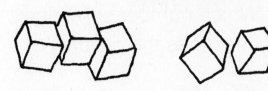

Ⓐ 3 + 3

Ⓑ 3 + 2

Ⓒ 1 + 4

Ⓓ 2 + 2

2. Ron has 6 marbles in all.
Some of the marbles are big.
4 of the marbles are small.
How many marbles are big?

Ⓐ 10

Ⓑ 5

Ⓒ 3

Ⓓ 2

3. Complete the picture to solve.
Write an addition sentence to show how many in all.

Miles has 1 pet.
Julia has 6 pets.
How many pets do they have altogether?

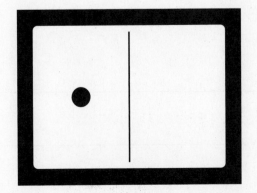

_____ + _____ = _____

Q 1·5

1. Which number sentence describes the picture?

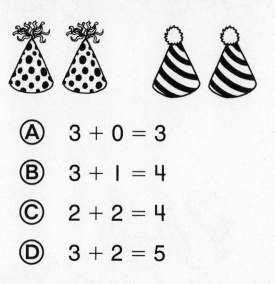

Ⓐ 3 + 0 = 3

Ⓑ 3 + 1 = 4

Ⓒ 2 + 2 = 4

Ⓓ 3 + 2 = 5

2. 2 children play tag. Then 4 more children join them. Which shows how many children there are now?

Ⓐ 2 + 6 = 8

Ⓑ 2 + 4 = 6

Ⓒ 2 + 3 = 5

Ⓓ 2 + 2 = 4

3. Writing in Math Use words and numbers to write a joining story about the frogs. Then write an addition sentence to show how many in all.

_____ + _____ = _____

_____

_____

_____

1. Which number sentences tell about the counters?

Ⓐ   3 + 3 = 6   4 + 2 = 6

Ⓑ   3 + 4 = 7   4 + 3 = 7

Ⓒ   4 + 4 = 8   5 + 3 = 8

Ⓓ   7 + 2 = 9   6 + 3 = 9

2. Kevin has 4 pennies in his left pocket.
He has the same number of pennies
in his right pocket.
How many pennies are in Kevin's pockets
in all?

Ⓐ   10

Ⓑ   8

Ⓒ   6

Ⓓ   4

3. Complete the picture to solve.
Write the number sentences.

Marni has some hair ribbons.
She has 7 pink ribbons.
The rest are purple ribbons.
She has 10 hair ribbons in all.

_____ + _____ = _____

_____ + _____ = _____

1. Annie puts 7 counters into two piles.
She puts 2 counters in one pile.
Which shows the number of counters
Annie puts in the other pile?

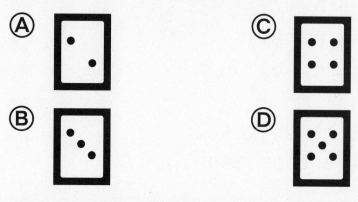

Ⓐ   Ⓒ

Ⓑ   Ⓓ

2. Which model shows one way to make 8?

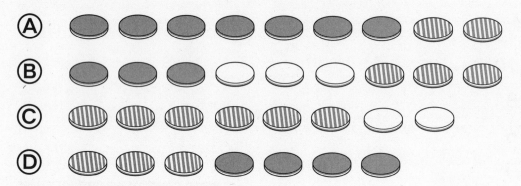

Ⓐ

Ⓑ

Ⓒ

Ⓓ

3. Use objects or draw a picture to solve.
Write the number sentences.

Enrique has 9 marbles.
He keeps some marbles.
He gives some to Brittany.

Show 2 ways Enrique and
Brittany can have the marbles.

____ + ____ = 9   ____ + ____ = 9

Q 1•8

1. Which shows the missing part of 7?

7	3	
whole	part	missing
	I know	part

Ⓐ ○○

Ⓑ ○○○

Ⓒ ○○○○

Ⓓ ○○○○○○○○○

2. Cara sees 4 birds in a tree.
   Desi sees some birds on a fence.
   Cara and Desi see 6 birds in all.
   How many birds does Desi see?

   Ⓐ 10

   Ⓑ 6

   Ⓒ 2

   Ⓓ 1

3. Draw a picture to solve.
   Write the numbers.

   There are 7 flowers in the vase.
   Some of the flowers are yellow
   and the rest are red.
   How many flowers are red?
   How many flowers are yellow?

   _____ red flowers

   _____ yellow flowers

Q 2·1

1. There are 8 counters in all.
5 counters are outside the bag.
Some counters are in the bag.
Which shows how many
counters are in the bag?

Ⓐ $8 - 5 = 3$

Ⓑ $8 - 2 = 6$

Ⓒ $8 - 1 = 7$

Ⓓ $8 - 0 = 8$

2. There are 8 cups on the shelf.
2 cups are broken.
How many cups are not broken?

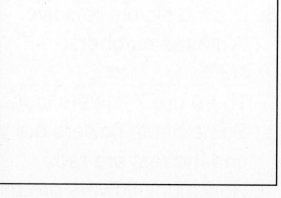

Ⓐ 10   Ⓒ 6

Ⓑ 7   Ⓓ 5

3. Draw a picture to solve.
Write the numbers.

There are 8 eggs in the carton.
Some eggs are white.
Some eggs are brown.
How many eggs are white?
How many eggs are brown?

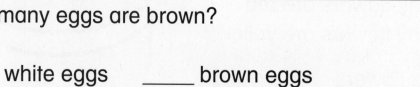

_____ white eggs   _____ brown eggs

1. Yani sees 9 ducks.
Some ducks are on the land.
5 ducks are in the water.
How many ducks are on
the land?

Ⓐ 9

Ⓑ 5

Ⓒ 4

Ⓓ 3

2. Which picture shows the missing part?

Ⓐ ●●●

Ⓑ ●●●●

Ⓒ ●●●●●

Ⓓ ●●●●●●●

3. Draw a picture to solve.
Write the number.

There are 9 dolls on the shelf.
Some dolls have black hair.
Some dolls have red hair.

_____ dolls have black hair.

_____ dolls have red hair.

Name _____

1. Which one tells about the model?

   Ⓐ 7 – 1

   Ⓑ 7 – 4

   Ⓒ 7 – 5

   Ⓓ 7 – 6

2. José has 8 grapes.
He gives 4 grapes to Tina.
How many grapes does
José have now?

   Ⓐ 2

   Ⓑ 4

   Ⓒ 8

   Ⓓ 12

3. Write a story about the ladybugs.
Use words and numbers.
Then write a subtraction sentence
to show how many are left.

_____

_____

_____ – _____ = _____

Name _____

1. Stan's mother has 6 apples.
She gives 2 apples to Stan.
How many apples does Stan's
mother have left?

(A) 4

(B) 3

(C) 2

(D) 1

2. Which number sentence
tells how many kittens
are in the basket?

(A) 2 − 2 = 0

(B) 3 − 2 = 1

(C) 4 − 2 = 2

(D) 5 − 3 = 2

3. Draw a picture to solve.
Write a subtraction sentence.

8 children are in the pool.
Then some children get out.
How many children are still
in the pool?

____ − ____ = ____

Q2·5

1. How many more apples are there than oranges?

Ⓐ 2

Ⓑ 3

Ⓒ 5

Ⓓ 11

2. Which number sentence tells how many more cars than bikes? _____

Ⓐ 9 − 3 = 6

Ⓑ 6 − 2 = 4

Ⓒ 9 − 6 = 3

Ⓓ 6 − 3 = 3

3. Use words and numbers to write a story about the balls. Then write a subtraction sentence to tell how many more balls.

_____

_____

_____ − _____ = _____ balls

1. Nick has 8 toy cars.
Some cars are blue.
3 cars are red.
How many cars are blue?

⒜ 3   © 8

Ⓑ 5   Ⓓ 11

2. Sara has 9 balls. 4 are tennis balls.
The rest are baseballs.
How many baseballs does Sara have?
Use cubes to help.

⒜ 12

Ⓑ 9

© 5

Ⓓ 4

3. Use the subtraction sentence $7 - 6 = 1$
to write a story about a missing part.
Label the whole and the parts in your story.

_____

_____

____ – ____ = ____
Whole   Part   Part

1. There were 9 ladybugs on a branch.
3 flew away.
How many ladybugs are left?

(A) 3   (C) 9

(B) 6   (D) 12

2. There are 5 turtles on a beach.
There are 3 turtles in the water.
Which number sentence tells how
many more turtles are on the beach
than in the water?

(A) $8 - 5 = 3$

(B) $3 + 1 = 4$

(C) $5 - 3 = 2$

(D) $5 + 3 = 8$

3. Draw a picture to solve.
Write the subtraction sentence.

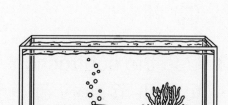

Sam has 6 fish in his tank.
Some fish are big and some fish are small.
If 4 fish are big, how many fish are small?

_____ − _____ = _____

_____ small fish

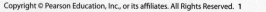

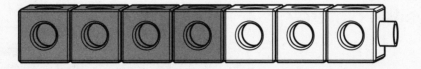

1. Which addition sentence tells about the picture?

Ⓐ $6 - 3 = 3$

Ⓑ $7 - 3 = 4$

Ⓒ $4 + 3 = 7$

Ⓓ $6 + 1 = 7$

2. Which subtraction sentence tells about the picture?

Ⓐ $5 + 2 = 7$

Ⓑ $4 + 3 = 7$

Ⓒ $7 - 4 = 3$

Ⓓ $6 - 3 = 3$

3. Draw a picture to solve. Write an addition sentence and a subtraction sentence.

There are 5 friends at Sam's birthday party. Some friends are girls. Some friends are boys. How many girls and boys are at the party?

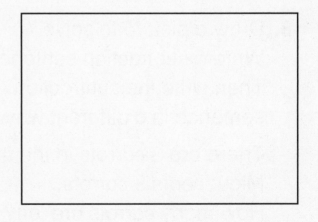

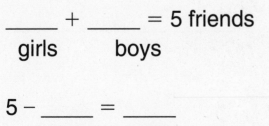

_____ + _____ = 5 friends
girls   boys

$5 -$ _____ $=$ _____
    boys   girls

1. Which number sentence matches the picture?

Ⓐ 4 = 7 – 3

Ⓑ 1 = 3 – 4

Ⓒ 5 – 3 = 2

Ⓓ 7 = 4 – 3

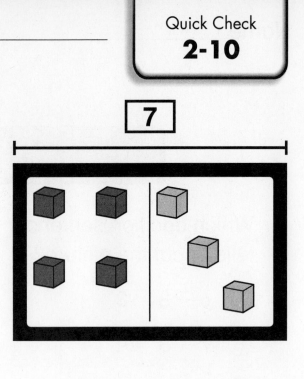

2. Which number sentence tells about the picture?

Ⓐ 6 – 3 = 3

Ⓑ 5 – 3 = 2

Ⓒ 3 = 6 – 3

Ⓓ 2 – 5 = 3

3. Draw a picture to solve.
Write a subtraction sentence.
Then write the subtraction
sentence in a different way.

There are 8 carrots in the fridge.
Miguel eats 3 carrots.
How many carrots are left?

_____ carrots

_____ – _____ = _____

_____ = _____ – _____

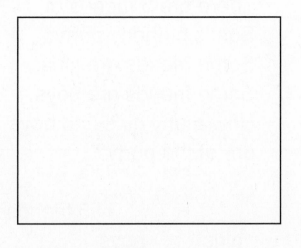

Name _____

1. There are 3 dinosaurs on a hill.
2 climb down.
How many dinosaurs are
on the hill now?

Ⓐ 1

Ⓑ 2

Ⓒ 3

Ⓓ 5

2. Which number sentence
tells about the picture?

Ⓐ 7 + 2 = 9

Ⓑ 6 + 1 = 7

Ⓒ 7 − 2 = 5

Ⓓ 7 − 7 = 0

3. Writing in Math

Write a story about the turtles.
Use words and numbers.
Write a subtraction sentence
to show how many are left.

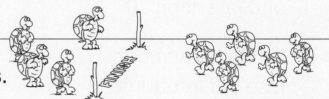

_____

_____

_____

_____ − _____ = _____

Name _____

1. Which number tells how many?

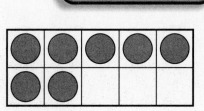

   Ⓐ 3

   Ⓑ 5

   Ⓒ 6

   Ⓓ 7

2. Lesli puts 4 counters in a ten-frame. How many more counters should she put in the frame to show 10?

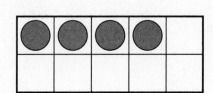

   Ⓐ 7

   Ⓑ 6

   Ⓒ 5

   Ⓓ 4

3. Pick a number greater than 5 and less than 10.

Write the number.
Use the ten-frame to show your number.

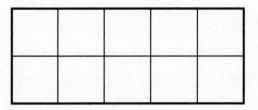

 Q 3·1

1. Which number is shown on the ten-frame?

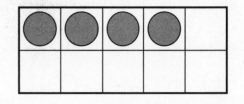

Ⓐ 9

Ⓑ 7

Ⓒ 5

Ⓓ 4

2. Tamika wrote about the ten-frame.
What did Tamika write?

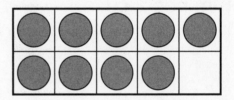

Ⓐ 5 and 3 is 8.

Ⓑ 2 away from 10 is 8.

Ⓒ 1 away from 10 is 9.

Ⓓ 1 more than 10 is 11.

3. Draw a picture to solve the problem.
Write the numbers.

Amy has some counters.
Tad has more counters than Amy.
The number of counters they have
in all is 2 away from 10.

Amy has _____ counters.

Tad has _____ counters.

1. 10 is 3 and _____.
Which is the missing number?

Ⓐ 5

Ⓑ 6

Ⓒ 7

Ⓓ 8

2. Kim and Karl have 10 cups in all.
Kim has 2 cups.
How many cups does Karl have?

Ⓐ 10

Ⓑ 9

Ⓒ 8

Ⓓ 2

3. Writing in Math
Draw a picture to solve.
Write the numbers.

Pedro has 10 beads.
Some beads are round
and some are square.
He has more than 3 square beads.

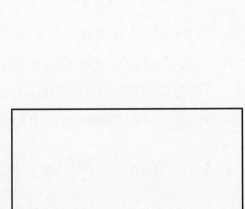

10 is _____ round beads and _____ square beads.

1. Which shows the missing part?

Ⓐ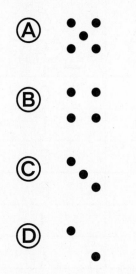

Ⓑ

Ⓒ

Ⓓ

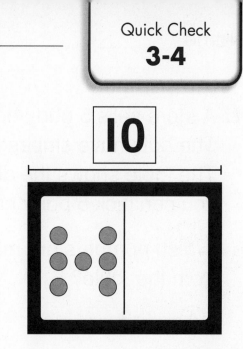

2. Kyra sees 10 bugs.
4 are black. The rest have spots.
How many bugs have spots?

Ⓐ 3

Ⓑ 4

Ⓒ 5

Ⓓ 6

3. Complete the picture to solve.
Then write the numbers.

Tali has 10 pencils.
Some are green.
1 pencil is blue.
How many pencils are green?

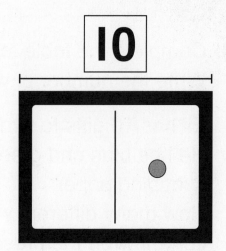

_____   _____
missing part   part I know

Q 3·4

I. A store sells 5 party hats for $1. The hats have stripes or polka dots. The table shows the different ways you can pick 5 party hats.

Which numbers are missing from the table?

Ⓐ 1, 3

Ⓑ 1, 5

Ⓒ 0, 4

Ⓓ 0, 5

5	0
4	1
3	2
2	3
1	4
?	?

2. How many different ways can you pick the 5 party hats?

Ⓐ 5

Ⓑ 6

Ⓒ 7

Ⓓ 8

3. Complete the table to solve. Write the number of ways.

Eli has 10 gifts to wrap. He has blue and green wrapping paper. How many different ways can Eli wrap the presents?

_____ different ways

Blue Paper	Green Paper
10	0

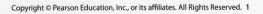

1. Which shows 1 more than 5?

Ⓐ

Ⓑ

Ⓒ

Ⓓ

2. Lee finds 7 maple leaves.
Then he finds 2 more.
How many maple leaves
does Lee find in all?

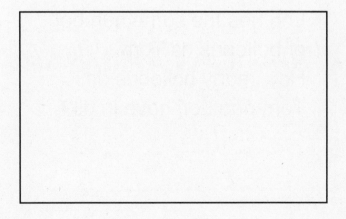

Ⓐ 7

Ⓑ 8

Ⓒ 9

Ⓓ 10

3. Draw a picture to solve.
Write the numbers.

Benji is 1 year older
than Simon.
Simon is 2 years older
than Annette.
Annette and Gordon are
the same age.
Gordon is 5 years old.

_____ _____ _____ _____
Benji   Simon   Annette   Gordon

1. Which is a doubles fact?

  Ⓐ 6 + 2 = 8

  Ⓑ 3 + 3 = 6

  Ⓒ 3 + 2 = 5

  Ⓓ 3 − 3 = 0

2. Ima has 2 bowls.
   She puts 5 cherries in each bowl.
   How many cherries in all?

  Ⓐ 2

  Ⓑ 5

  Ⓒ 7

  Ⓓ 10

3. Draw a picture to solve.
   Write an addition sentence.

   Tom has some balloons.
   Lori has the same number
   of balloons as Tom.
   How many balloons do
   Tom and Lori have in all?

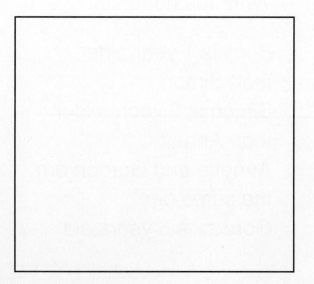

_____ + _____ = _____

1. Which shows a near double?

Ⓐ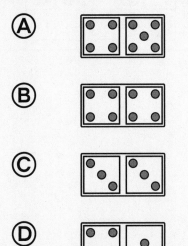

Ⓑ

Ⓒ

Ⓓ

2. Maria saw 3 butterflies.
Juana saw 1 more than Maria.
How many butterflies
did they see in all?

Ⓐ 4

Ⓑ 5

Ⓒ 6

Ⓓ 7

3. Draw a picture to solve.
Write an addition sentence.

Tammy picked some flowers.
Gil picked 1 more flower
than Tammy.
How many flowers did they
pick in all?

_____ + _____ = _____

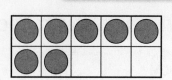

1. Which tells about the ten-frame?

   Ⓐ $5 + 0 = 5$

   Ⓑ $10 - 5 = 5$

   Ⓒ $5 + 2 = 7$

   Ⓓ $5 + 3 = 8$

2. Which is the missing number?

   $7 + \underline{\hspace{2cm}} = 10$

   Ⓐ   5

   Ⓑ   4

   Ⓒ   3

   Ⓓ   2

3. Writing in Math

Draw a picture to solve.
Write an addition sentence.

Sara's camp has 5 tents.
The campers set up
2 more tents.
How many tents does
Sara's camp have now?

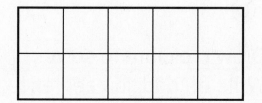

$\underline{\hspace{2cm}} + \underline{\hspace{2cm}} = \underline{\hspace{2cm}}$

Name _____

1. If 6 + 6 = 12, then 12 − 6 = ☐.
Which shows the missing number?

Ⓐ 12

Ⓑ 7

Ⓒ 6

Ⓓ 5

2. Connie has 8 pennies.
She puts 4 pennies in her purse.
How many pennies are left?

Ⓐ 0

Ⓑ 4

Ⓒ 8

Ⓓ 12

3. Draw dot patterns to solve.
Write the number sentences.

Quincy and Quinn are twins.
Each has the same number
of books.
How many books do the twins
have in all?

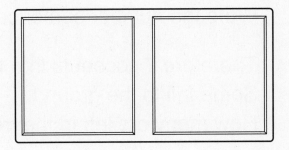

_____ + _____ = _____

_____ − _____ = _____

Q 4·7

I. Write the missing part. Which subtraction
sentence matches the picture?

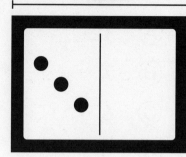

Ⓐ   13 – 5 = 8

Ⓑ   8 – 3 = 5

Ⓒ   5 – 2 = 3

Ⓓ   8 – 6 = 2

2. Ellie has 9 stones.
She uses 6 to make a pattern.
Which addition fact can help
you find how many stones
Ellie has left?

Ⓐ   3 + 3 = 6

Ⓑ   6 + 3 = 9

Ⓒ   9 + 3 = 12

Ⓓ   9 + 6 = 15

3. Complete the picture to solve.
Write the number sentences.

There are 7 coconuts in a tree.
Some fall to the ground.
How many are left in the tree?

_____ + _____ = _____

_____ – _____ = _____

1. Write the missing part. Which number sentences match the picture?

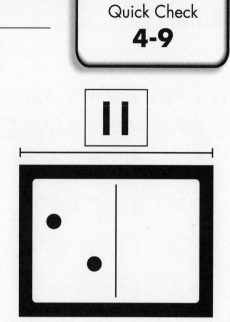

Ⓐ 2 + 9 = 11. So, 11 − 2 = 9.

Ⓑ 2 + 7 = 9. So, 9 − 2 = 7.

Ⓒ 2 + 2 = 4. So, 4 − 2 = 2.

Ⓓ 2 + 11 = 13. So, 13 − 2 = 11.

2. Which number makes both facts true?

12 − 7 = _____   7 + _____ = 12

Ⓐ 19

Ⓑ 7

Ⓒ 6

Ⓓ 5

3. Complete the picture to solve.
Write the number sentences.

Madison sees 12 bears at the zoo.
Some are brown.
The rest are white.

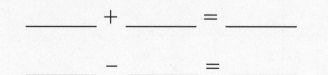

Name _____

1. Which addition sentence
tells about the picture?

Ⓐ   7 + 2 = 9

Ⓑ   8 + 2 = 10

Ⓒ   10 + 2 = 12

Ⓓ   10 + 8 = 18

2. Richie takes 9 pictures.
Alice takes 3 pictures.
Which shows how many more
pictures Richie takes than Alice?

Ⓐ   12 − 3 = 9

Ⓑ   9 − 3 = 6

Ⓒ   12 − 9 = 3

Ⓓ   9 − 6 = 3

3. Write a number sentence
to solve.
Draw a picture to check.

There are 4 beach towels
on the sand.
Tracey sets up more towels.
How many beach towels are
there now?

_____ + _____ = _____

Q 4·10

Name _____

1. Which doubles fact
   does the picture show?

   Ⓐ   3 + 3 = 6

   Ⓑ   4 + 4 = 8

   Ⓒ   5 + 5 = 10

   Ⓓ   6 + 6 = 12

2. Donna has the same number
   of pennies as Dominick.
   They have 18 pennies in all.
   How many pennies does
   Donna have?

   Ⓐ   18

   Ⓑ   11

   Ⓒ   9

   Ⓓ   8

3. Complete the picture to solve the problem.
   Write the doubles fact.

   Corrina reads some pages of her
   book on Monday. She reads the
   same number of pages on Tuesday.
   Tell the number of pages Corrina
   reads in all.

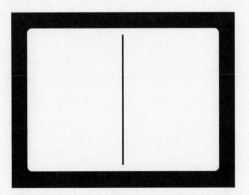

_____ = _____ + _____

1. Which doubles-plus-1 fact does the picture show?

   Ⓐ $6 + 1 = 7$

   Ⓑ $7 + 3 = 10$

   Ⓒ $6 + 6 = 12$

   Ⓓ $6 + 7 = 13$

2. Which would you use to solve $9 + 8$?

   Ⓐ $7 + 7$ and 1 more

   Ⓑ $8 + 8$ and 1 more

   Ⓒ $8 + 8$ and 2 more

   Ⓓ $9 + 9$ and 1 more

3. **Writing in Math**

   Use words and numbers to write a story about the chicks. Then write an addition sentence to show how many in all.

   _____

   _____

   _____

   _____ + _____ = _____ chicks

1. Which doubles-plus-2 fact does the picture show?

  Ⓐ   5 + 5 = 10

  Ⓑ   5 + 7 = 12

  Ⓒ   6 + 8 = 14

  Ⓓ   7 + 7 = 14

2. Which would you use to solve 9 + 11?

  Ⓐ   9 + 9 and 1 more

  Ⓑ   9 + 9 and 2 more

  Ⓒ   10 + 10 and 1 more

  Ⓓ   10 + 10 and 2 more

3. Draw a picture to solve. Write an addition sentence to show how many in all.

Tonya and Cort fed the same number of goats at the zoo. Then Cort fed 2 more goats.

How many goats did they feed in all?

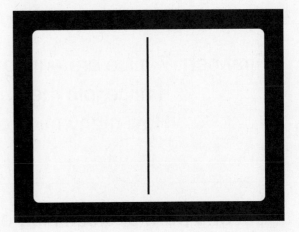

_____ + _____ = _____ goats

Name _____

1. 8 monkeys are in a tree. 5 monkeys climb down. 3 monkeys climb up. How many monkeys are in the tree now? Which number sentence shows the first part?

    Ⓐ $8 - 5 = 3$

    Ⓑ $5 + 3 = 8$

    Ⓒ $13 - 5 = 8$

    Ⓓ $13 - 3 = 10$

2. 10 students are in Mr. Patel's class. 3 students join his class. 1 student moves to a different class. How many students are in Mr. Patel's class now? Which number sentence solves the second part?

    Ⓐ $13 - 1 = 12$

    Ⓑ $10 - 1 = 9$

    Ⓒ $10 - 3 = 7$

    Ⓓ $10 - 4 = 6$

3. Write a number sentence to solve each part.

First part: 7 mice are eating some cheese.
          4 mice join them.
          How many mice are eating cheese?

_____ ◯ _____ = _____

Second part: 5 mice finish eating and leave.
          How many mice are still eating?

_____ ◯ _____ = _____

1. Which completes the number sentence?

9 + 6 = 10 + _____ = 15

Ⓐ 9   Ⓒ 6

Ⓑ 8   Ⓓ 5

2. Selena wrote 7 valentines.
Ron wrote 6 valentines.
Which addition fact can help you find
how many valentines in all?

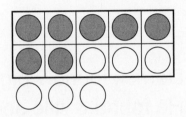

Ⓐ 10 + 7 = 17   Ⓒ 10 + 4 = 14

Ⓑ 10 + 6 = 16   Ⓓ 10 + 3 = 13

3. Pick 2 numbers from the box.

Draw a picture to show
how you would make a 10
to add the numbers you
picked. Then write 2 addition
sentences.

10 + _____ = _____

_____ + _____ = _____

| 5 | 6 | 7 | 8 | 9 |

Name _____

1. Which completes the number sentence?

9 + 4 = 10 + _____ = 13

Ⓐ 5

Ⓑ 4

Ⓒ 3

Ⓓ 2

2. Derrick found 9 big seashells.
He found 6 little seashells.
How many more counters do you need
to show how many seashells in all?

Ⓐ

Ⓑ

Ⓒ

Ⓓ

3. Writing in Math

Pick 1 number from the box.

| 5 | 6 | 7 | 8 | 9 |

Use words, numbers, or pictures
to tell how you would make a 10
to add 9 to the number
you picked.

Then write 2 addition sentences.

10 + _____ = _____

_____ + 9 = _____

Q 5·6

Name _____

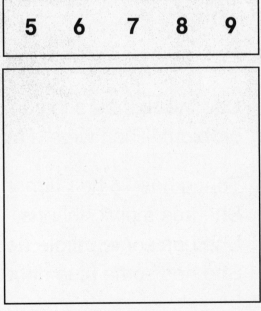

1. Bob blew up 8 blue balloons.
Jane blew up 9 red balloons.
How many more counters do you
need to show how many balloons in all?

  Ⓐ 9

  Ⓑ 8

  Ⓒ 7

  Ⓓ 1

2. Which 2 facts have the same sum?

  Ⓐ 10 + 4 and 8 + 6

  Ⓑ 10 + 6 and 8 + 6

  Ⓒ 10 + 8 and 8 + 9

  Ⓓ 10 + 7 and 8 + 8

3. Writing in Math

Pick 1 number from the box.

5	6	7	8	9

Use words, numbers, or
pictures to tell how you
would make a 10 to add 8 to
the number you picked.

Then write 2 addition sentences.

10 + _____ = _____

_____ + 8 = _____

I. José collects toy cars.
   He has 5 red, 3 yellow, and 5 green cars.
   How many cars does José have in all?

   (A) 5

   (B) 8

   (C) 10

   (D) 13

2. Aaron needs 16 hats for his party.
   He bought 3 on Monday.
   He bought 5 more on Tuesday.
   How many more hats does Aaron need?

   (A) 13

   (B) 11

   (C) 8

   (D) 6

3. Pick 2 numbers from the box. | 2 3 4 5 6 7 8 |

   Use the numbers to complete the picture and solve the
   problem. Then write a number sentence.

   Tonya has 16 hair ribbons in all.
   She has 6 pink ribbons.
   She has some purple ribbons.
   She has some blue ribbons.

   _____ + 6 + _____ = 16

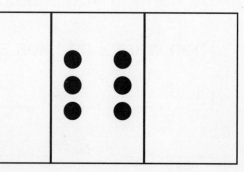

Name _____

I. Tarik has some toy cars.
He has 2 green cars, 6 blue cars, and 4 red cars.
Which number sentence shows how many cars he has
in all?

Ⓐ $2 + 6 = 8$

Ⓑ $2 + 6 + 4 = 12$

Ⓒ $2 + 6 + 6 = 14$

Ⓓ $8 + 10 = 18$

2. Mia has some markers.
She has 7 red markers, 7 blue markers,
and 2 orange markers.
How many markers does she have in all?

Ⓐ   12   Ⓒ   15

Ⓑ   14   Ⓓ   16

3. Jo has more than 10 buttons.
She has fewer than 20 buttons.
She puts some buttons in each box.
Draw the buttons. Then write the number sentence to show
how many she has in all.

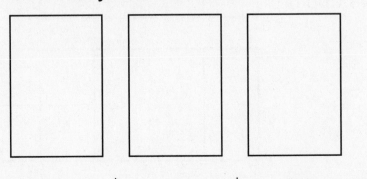

_____ + _____ + _____ = _____

Name _____

1. Make a 10 to subtract.

15 − 7 = ?

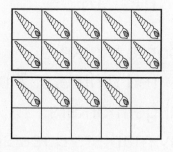

Ⓐ 7

Ⓑ 8

Ⓒ 9

Ⓓ 10

2. Rita has 14 shells.
She hides 9 in the sand.
How many shells are left?

Ⓐ 10

Ⓑ 9

Ⓒ 5

Ⓓ 4

3. Make a 10 to solve.
17 cats are in the yard.
8 cats are napping.
How many cats are not napping?

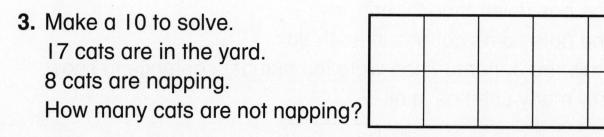

17 − _____ = 10

10 − _____ = _____

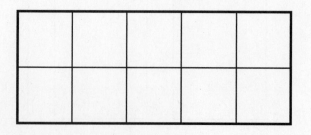

1. There are 12 cows in the barn.
Then 5 cows go away.
How many cows
are left in the barn?

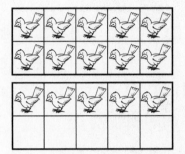

Ⓐ 7   Ⓒ 3

Ⓑ 5   Ⓓ 2

2. Ray sees 15 birds in the tree.
If 8 birds fly away, how
many birds are left in the tree?
Choose the subtraction sentence
that shows the story.

Ⓐ 15 − 7 = 8   Ⓒ 10 − 4 = 6

Ⓑ 15 − 8 = 7   Ⓓ 10 − 6 = 4

3. Joseph had 14 stickers.
He gave some stickers away.
How many stickers does
Joseph have left?

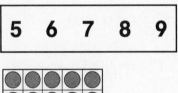

Pick a number from the box to
show how many stickers Joseph
gave away. Show how you would
make a 10 to subtract your number
from 14.

Then write the subtraction sentence.

14 − ____ = ____

Name _____

I. Which is the whole?

6 + 8 = _____

Ⓐ 6

Ⓑ 8

Ⓒ 10

Ⓓ 14

2. Kyle wrote the addition sentence 7 + 4 = 11 for the picture. Which subtraction sentence is related?

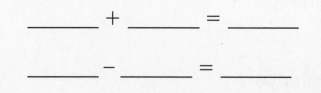

Ⓐ 11 − 6 = 5

Ⓑ 11 − 7 = 4

Ⓒ 7 − 4 = 3

Ⓓ 4 − 4 = 0

3. Complete the picture to solve. Write the number sentences.

Michael sees 17 caterpillars.
Some are brown.
The rest are green.

_____ + _____ = _____

_____ − _____ = _____

1. Which part of the fact family is missing?
   $14 = 6 + 8$ $14 = 8 + 6$ $6 = 14 - 8$

   Ⓐ $6 = 16 - 10$

   Ⓑ $14 = 10 - 4$

   Ⓒ $14 = 5 + 9$

   Ⓓ $8 = 14 - 6$

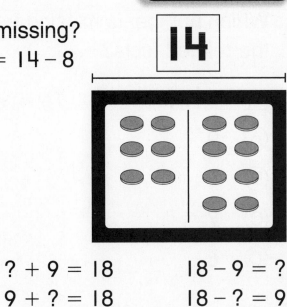

14

2. Which number completes
   the fact family?

   $? + 9 = 18$ $18 - 9 = ?$
   $9 + ? = 18$ $18 - ? = 9$

   7   8   11   9
   Ⓐ   Ⓑ   Ⓒ   Ⓓ

3. Complete the model to solve.
   Write the subtraction sentence.
   Then write the fact family.

15

   Kendra scored 15 points in all.
   In the first half, she scored 6 points.
   How many points did Kendra score
   in the second half?

   _____ – _____ = _____

   Complete the fact family.

   _____ + _____ = _____

   _____ + _____ = _____

   _____ – _____ = _____

Q 6·4

I. Which number is missing from
the related facts?

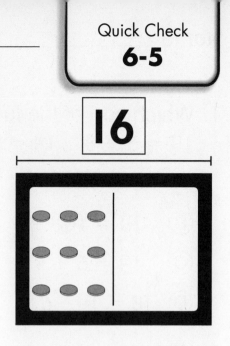

16

_____ = 16 − 9   16 = 9 + _____

Ⓐ 9

Ⓑ 8

Ⓒ 7

Ⓓ 6

2. Josh has 18 peanuts.
He feeds 6 peanuts to a squirrel.
Which addition fact can help you
find how many peanuts Josh has left?

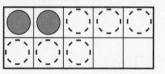

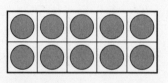

Ⓐ   18 − 9 = 9

Ⓑ   10 + 2 = 12

Ⓒ   6 + 10 = 16

Ⓓ   12 + 6 = 18

3. Writing in Math Use words and
numbers to write a story about
the flowers.
Write a subtraction sentence
to tell how many flowers are left.
Then write an addition fact
you could use to solve it.

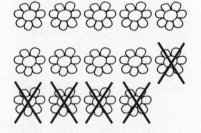

_____ − _____ = _____ flowers   _____

_____ + _____ = _____ flowers   _____

1. Omar solved a subtraction problem.
   He used $13 + 7 = 20$ to help him solve it.
   Which subtraction problem did Omar solve?

   (A) $20 - 7 = 13$

   (B) $14 - 7 = 7$

   (C) $20 - 11 = 9$

   (D) $11 - 7 = 4$

2. Zoe has 17 raisins. She eats 8 of them.
   Which related sentences can help you
   find how many raisins are left?

   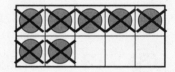
   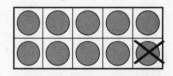

   (A) $9 + 8 = 17$ and $17 - 8 = 9$

   (B) $8 + 7 = 15$ and $15 - 7 = 8$

   (C) $9 + 1 = 10$ and $10 - 1 = 9$

   (D) $8 - 1 = 7$ and $7 + 1 = 8$

3. **Writing to Explain**
   Use words and numbers to
   write a story about the teddy bears.
   Write a subtraction sentence
   that matches your story.
   Then write an addition fact
   you could use to solve it.

   _____ − _____ = _____ teddy bears

   _____ + _____ = _____ teddy bears

Name _____

1. Which subtraction sentence matches the picture?

   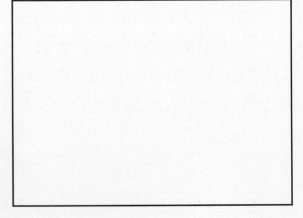

   Ⓐ 15 − 7 = 8

   Ⓑ 14 − 7 = 7

   Ⓒ 13 − 7 = 6

   Ⓓ 7 − 7 = 0

2. Ned has 5 toy boats.
   Valerie has 7 toy boats.
   Which number sentence
   tells how many toy boats in all?

   Ⓐ 12 − 8 = 4

   Ⓑ 12 − 7 = 5

   Ⓒ 5 + 7 = 12

   Ⓓ 6 + 7 = 13

3. Write a number sentence to solve.
   Draw a picture to check.

   Sylvia has 16 pennies
   in her pocket.
   She buys a muffin
   that costs 9 pennies.
   How many pennies does
   Sylvia have left?

   _____ ◯ _____ = _____

Q 6•7

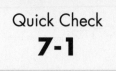

1. Which shows 15?

Ⓐ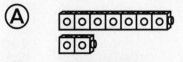

Ⓑ

Ⓒ

Ⓓ

2. Which numbers make 18?

Ⓐ   11 and 8

Ⓑ   10 and 6

Ⓒ   10 and 8

Ⓓ   8 and 9

3. Draw a picture to solve.
Write the numbers.

A box can hold 18 dominoes.
There are 10 dominoes
in the box now.
How many more dominoes
can fit?

18 is _____ and _____ .

1. Which number is 3 fewer than 14?

Ⓐ 17

Ⓑ 13

Ⓒ 11

Ⓓ 7

2. Ray has 13 blocks.
Kelly has 15 blocks.
How many more blocks
does Kelly have than Ray?

Ⓐ 2

Ⓑ 3

Ⓒ 5

Ⓓ 10

3. Use the number line to solve.
Write the names under the numbers.
Then write the numbers in order.

Joy has some pencils.
Pam has 1 fewer pencil than Joy.
Will has 2 more pencils than Pam.

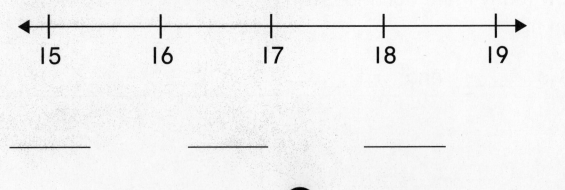

15   16   17   18   19

_____   _____   _____

1. Which number do
the ten-frames show?

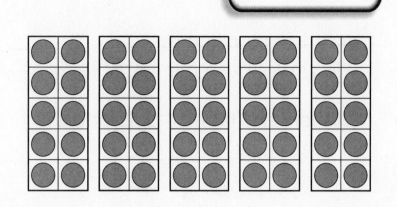

Ⓐ   5

Ⓑ   25

Ⓒ   40

Ⓓ   50

2. Juan has 4 toy trucks.
Each truck has 10 wheels.
How many wheels are there in all?

Ⓐ   40

Ⓑ   14

Ⓒ   10

Ⓓ   4

3. Writing in Math
Use words and numbers.
Write a story about the crayons.
Then write the number
of crayons in all.

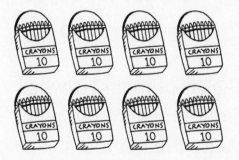

_____

_____

_____

There are _____ crayons in all.

I. Yoshi is counting by 1s.
He wrote these numbers: 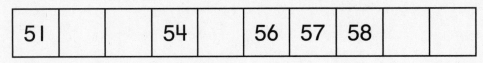 **63, 64, 65**.

Which are the next 3 numbers
Yoshi writes?

Ⓐ   64, 65, 66

Ⓑ   65, 64, 63

Ⓒ   65, 66, 67

Ⓓ   66, 67, 68

2. Which numbers are missing from this part of the hundred chart?

| 51 | | | 54 | | 56 | 57 | 58 | | |

Ⓐ   51, 53, 55, 59, 60

Ⓑ   52, 54, 56, 58, 60

Ⓒ   52, 53, 55, 59, 60

Ⓓ   62, 63, 65, 69, 70

3. Pick a number between 60 and 80.
Count forward by 1s.
Write the numbers.

_____, _____, _____, _____, _____, _____, _____

1. Micah skip counts to find the
number of pencils.
There are 10 pencils in each pack.
Which numbers does he say?

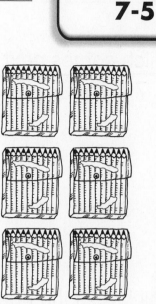

   Ⓐ   6, 7, 8, 9, 10, 11

   Ⓑ   6, 12, 18, 24, 30, 36

   Ⓒ   16, 18, 20, 22, 24, 26

   Ⓓ   10, 20, 30, 40, 50, 60

2. Jada has 3 vases.
She puts 5 flowers in each vase.
How many flowers in all?

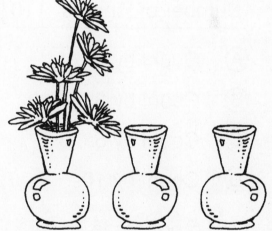

   Ⓐ   15

   Ⓑ   13

   Ⓒ   10

   Ⓓ   8

3. Draw a picture and use skip
counting to solve.
Write the numbers.

John sees some birds in the park.
He counts 18 wings in all.
How many birds does John see?

_____ birds

Name _____

I. Which comes next?

65, 70, 75, _____

Ⓐ 40

Ⓑ 70

Ⓒ 80

Ⓓ 100

2. Which tells the pattern in the table?

Number of Children	I	2	3	4	5	6
Number of Fingers	10	20	30	40	50	60

Ⓐ Count by 2s.

Ⓑ Count by 3s.

Ⓒ Count by 5s.

Ⓓ Count by 10s.

3. Find a pattern to solve.

Write the pattern. Then write the number.

Joan saves the same number of pennies each day.
At the end of a week, Joan has 35 pennies.
How many pennies does Joan save each day?

Number of Days	I	2	3	4	5	6	7
Number of Pennies		10		20			35

The pattern is count by _____s.

_____ pennies

Name _____

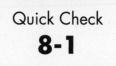

1. Which number is 1 group of ten and 4 left over?

Ⓐ 5

Ⓑ 14

Ⓒ 21

Ⓓ 41

2. Which number is shown?

Ⓐ 37

Ⓑ 27

Ⓒ 17

Ⓓ 15

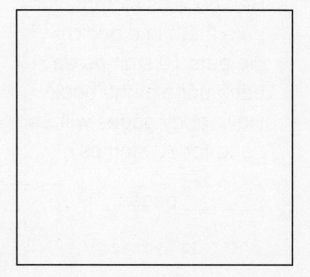

3. Draw a picture to solve.
Write the numbers that show
how many pencils Tammy put
in her case and how many
she put in her desk.

Tammy has 37 pencils.
She puts each group of
10 pencils in her pencil case.
She puts the leftover pencils
in her desk.

_____ in case

_____ in desk

Name _____

1. Which is the missing number that completes the pattern?

30, 40, 50, 60, _____, 80, 90

Ⓐ 70

Ⓑ 20

Ⓒ 17

Ⓓ 10

2. Which shows that 5 tens is 50?

Ⓐ ▭▭ ▭▭

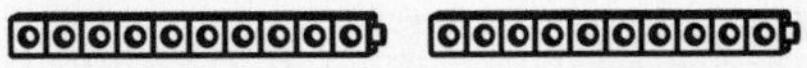

Ⓑ ▭▭ ▭▭ ▭▭

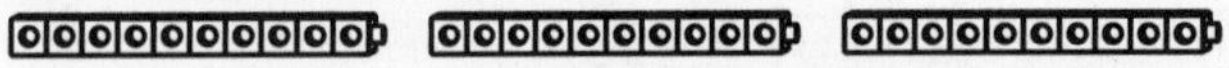

Ⓒ ▭▭ ▭▭ ▭▭ ▭▭

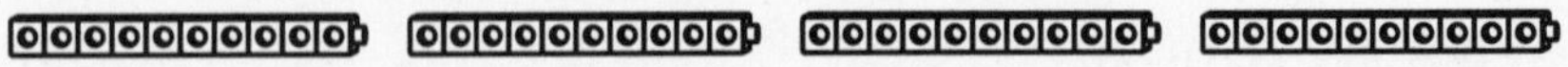

Ⓓ ▭▭ ▭▭ ▭▭ ▭▭ ▭▭

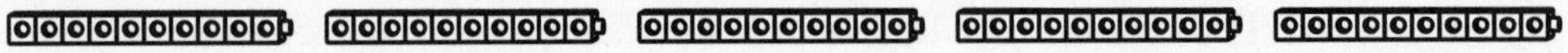

3. Draw a picture to solve.
Write the number.

Ben collects stamps and puts them in a book. He puts 10 stamps on each page of the book. How many pages will Ben need for 70 stamps?

_____ pages

1. Which number does the picture show?

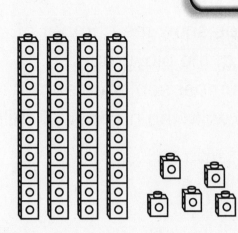

Ⓐ 45

Ⓑ 35

Ⓒ 15

Ⓓ 9

2. Which is the missing number?

_____ tens and 7 ones is the same as 47.

Ⓐ 4

Ⓑ 5

Ⓒ 7

Ⓓ 11

3. Writing in Math

Draw a picture to solve.
Explain your answer.

Sara is assigned to bring
48 juice boxes to the party.
Each package holds
10 juice boxes.
Sara says she needs to buy
5 packages.
Is Sara correct?

_____

_____

1. The cubes show the number of
   children at the playground.
   Which number sentence shows
   a way to write the number of children?

Tens	Ones

   (A)   4 + 6 = 10

   (B)   10 + 6 = 16

   (C)   40 + 6 = 46

   (D)   60 + 4 = 64

2. Penelope has 57 crayons.
   Which is another way to write 57?

   (A)   7 tens + 5 ones

   (B)   6 tens + 7 ones

   (C)   5 tens + 7 ones

   (D)   3 tens + 4 ones

3. Choose a two-digit number
   that is less than 30.

   Draw the number as
   tens and ones.
   Complete the
   number sentence.

Tens	Ones

   _____ tens + _____ ones = _____

Name _____

1. Which of these is **not**
a way to show 65?

Ⓐ 2 tens   45 ones

Ⓑ 3 tens   35 ones

Ⓒ 4 tens   25 ones

Ⓓ 6 tens   15 ones

2. Which number does
the model show?

Ⓐ 26

Ⓑ 18

Ⓒ 16

Ⓓ 6

Tens	Ones

3. Draw a model to solve.
Write the addition sentences.

Stephen wants to show 21
as tens and ones.
What are all the ways
Stephen can make 21?

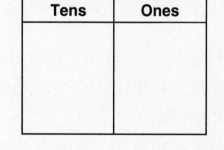

Tens	Ones

_____ + _____ = _____

_____ + _____ = _____

_____ + _____ = _____

Q 8·5

1. Greta's list shows some ways
to make 35.
She forgot 1 way.
Which numbers are missing
from her list?

Ⓐ   1 and 20

Ⓑ   1 and 25

Ⓒ   0 and 15

Ⓓ   2 and 35

Tens	Ones
0	35
2	15
3	5

2. Which number is shown?

Ⓐ   29

Ⓑ   20

Ⓒ   18

Ⓓ   11

Tens	Ones
1	19
2	9

3. Choose a number.
Make a list to solve the problem.

Fred picks a number that is
greater than 40 and less
than 50.
He wants to show his number
as tens and ones.
What are all the ways Fred can
make his number?

_____ Fred's number

Tens	Ones

1. Sam has 52 stamps.
   Eric has 1 more stamp than Sam.
   How many stamps does Eric have?

   Ⓐ 62

   Ⓑ 53

   Ⓒ 51

   Ⓓ 42

2. Which number is 10 less than
   the number shown?

   Ⓐ 25

   Ⓑ 35

   Ⓒ 45

   Ⓓ 55

3. Finish the clue about your secret number.
   Write your secret number.

   My secret number is between

   _____ and _____.

   It is 10 more than _____.

   It is 1 less than _____.

   My secret number is _____.

Name _____

1. Ping's farm has 37 animals.
   Kyle's farm has 10 less than Ping's.
   How many animals are on Kyle's farm?

   Ⓐ 47

   Ⓑ 38

   Ⓒ 36

   Ⓓ 27

2. There are 43 bees in the hive.
   10 more bees arrive. 1 bee leaves.
   If you start at 43 on the hundred chart, which directions
   do you go to find how many bees are in the hive now?

   Ⓐ down and left

   Ⓑ down and right

   Ⓒ up and left

   Ⓓ up and right

3. **Writing in Math** Write sentences to answer.

   If you start at a number on the hundred chart,
   what happens if you move 1 square to the left?

   _____

   _____

   If you start at a number on the hundred chart, what happens
   if you move 1 square up?

   _____

   _____

1. There are more than 23 penguins at the zoo. How many penguins could there be?

Ⓐ   13

Ⓑ   18

Ⓒ   21

Ⓓ   27

2. Which is true?

Ⓐ   39 < 32

Ⓑ   39 = 32

Ⓒ   39 > 32

Ⓓ   39 < 38

3. Write the numbers.
Then use <, >, or = to compare them.

Tonya has more than 60 comic books.
Allie has more than 60 comic books.
Allie has fewer comic books than Tonya.

Tonya has _____ comic books.

Allie has _____ comic books.

_____ ◯ _____
 Tonya   Allie

1. Which shows the numbers in order from least to greatest?

Ⓐ   67, 55, 79

Ⓑ   79, 67, 55

Ⓒ   55, 79, 67

Ⓓ   55, 67, 79

2. Fen has 48 crayons.
Sylvia has 96 crayons.
Betsy has the fewest crayons.

How many crayons can
Betsy have?

Ⓐ   120

Ⓑ   96

Ⓒ   64

Ⓓ   32

3. Write the numbers.
Put them in order from greatest to least.

Noah recycled 83 plastic bottles.
Allie recycled more bottles than Noah.
Ed recycled the least number of bottles.

Noah: 83 bottles   Allie: _____ bottles   Ed: _____ bottles

_____   _____   _____
greatest   least

Name _____

1. I am a number greater than 7 but less than 11.
You say my name when you count by 2s.
What number am I?

Ⓐ 11　　　Ⓒ 9

Ⓑ 10　　　Ⓓ 7

2. I am a girl. I am older
than 9. Who am I?

Ⓐ Becky

Ⓑ Gloria

Ⓒ Patrick

Ⓓ Nina

Becky	Gloria	Patrick
6 years	10 years	10 years
Nina	Ronald	Daniel
5 years	7 years	11 years

3. Make a list to solve.
Write the numbers.

A secret number is greater
than 44 and less than 51.
What number could it be?

You say the secret number
when you skip count by 5s.
What number could it be?

The secret number has
more tens than ones.

The secret number is _____.

Numbers
_____
_____
_____
_____
_____
_____
_____

Numbers
_____
_____

Q 9·5

1. Camden has 20 crayons.
Alice has 30 crayons.
Which addition sentence shows
how many crayons in all?

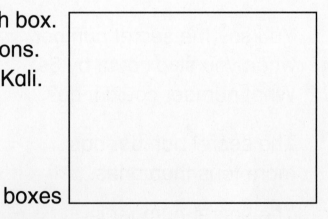

Ⓐ   20 + 3 = 23

Ⓑ   30 + 2 = 32

Ⓒ   20 + 20 = 40

Ⓓ   20 + 30 = 50

2. Which is the missing number?

30 + _____ = 80

Ⓐ   50

Ⓑ   40

Ⓒ   30

Ⓓ   10

3. Draw a picture to solve.
Then write the addition sentences.

There are 10 crayons in each box.
Kali has some boxes of crayons.
Jamal has more boxes than Kali.
Kali and Jamal have
80 crayons altogether.

_____ + _____ = _____ boxes

_____ + _____ = _____ crayons

1. Hans puts 24 books on
   a shelf.
   He puts 40 books on
   another shelf.
   How many books in all?

   Ⓐ 64

   Ⓑ 60

   Ⓒ 44

   Ⓓ 42

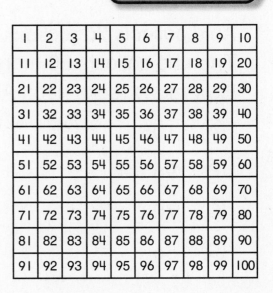

1	2	3	4	5	6	7	8	9	10
11	12	13	14	15	16	17	18	19	20
21	22	23	24	25	26	27	28	29	30
31	32	33	34	35	36	37	38	39	40
41	42	43	44	45	46	47	48	49	50
51	52	53	54	55	56	57	58	59	60
61	62	63	64	65	66	67	68	69	70
71	72	73	74	75	76	77	78	79	80
81	82	83	84	85	86	87	88	89	90
91	92	93	94	95	96	97	98	99	100

2. Gabby plants 37 flowers.
   Then she plants 30 more.
   Which addition sentence
   shows how many flowers in all?

   Ⓐ 7 + 30 = 37

   Ⓑ 37 + 3 = 40

   Ⓒ 37 + 30 = 67

   Ⓓ 40 + 30 = 70

3. Pick and circle a number on the
   hundred chart that is greater than
   50 and less than 80.

   Add 20 to your number.
   Complete the addition sentence.

   _____ + 20 = _____

Q 10·2

1. Abid collects 76 rocks.
   Then he collects 20 more.
   How many rocks does Abid have in all?

   Ⓐ 106

   Ⓑ 96

   Ⓒ 70

   Ⓓ 56

2. Violet buys 4 packs of 10 pencils.
   Harry gives Violet 13 more pencils.
   Which number sentence shows how
   many pencils Violet has altogether?

   Ⓐ $4 + 13 = 17$

   Ⓑ $10 + 13 = 23$

   Ⓒ $14 + 13 = 27$

   Ⓓ $40 + 13 = 53$

3. Pick a number greater
   than 45 and less than 60.
   Add 20, 30, or 40 to
   your number.

   Write a number sentence.

   _____ + _____ = _____

Add using mental math.
Use models if you need to.

1. Add using mental math. Which shows the sum?

   40 + 49 = _____

   Ⓐ 89

   Ⓑ 53

   Ⓒ 49

   Ⓓ 90

2. 16 bees buzz in the roses. 60 bees buzz in the tulips. How many bees buzz in all?

   Ⓐ 86

   Ⓑ 76

   Ⓒ 66

   Ⓓ 55

3. Choose a two-digit number from the box. Circle it. Write a story about adding 20 to your number.

29	17
43	35

   _____

   _____

   _____

   _____

   Complete the number sentence to show your addition.

   _____ + 20 = _____

Name _____

1. Which needs regrouping to add?

    Ⓐ   47 + 3

    Ⓑ   32 + 7

    Ⓒ   15 + 4

    Ⓓ   11 + 8

2. June had 54 marbles.
She bought 9 more.
How many marbles does June
have now?

    Ⓐ   59

    Ⓑ   62

    Ⓒ   63

    Ⓓ   73

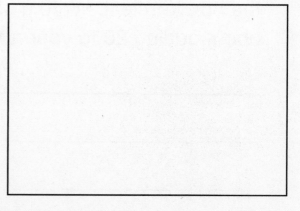

Tens	Ones

3. Draw a picture to solve.
Explain your answer.
Then write the sum.

Jessie has 15 T-shirts.
She buys 8 more T-shirts.
Jessie says she has to regroup
to find how many T-shirts
she has in all.
Is she correct?

_____

_____

Jessie has _____ T-shirts in all.

Q 10·5

1. Which number sentence shows the problem?

Ⓐ 8 − 5 = 3   Ⓒ 80 − 50 = 30

Ⓑ 8 − 3 = 5   Ⓓ 80 − 30 = 50

2. Subtract.
7 tens − 3 tens = _____?_____

Ⓐ 3   Ⓒ 30

Ⓑ 4   Ⓓ 40

3. Complete the number sentences to solve.
Write the answer.

Sarah had 50 stickers.
She gave 40 to her sister.
How many stickers does Sarah have left?

_____ tens − _____ tens = _____ ten

_____ − _____ = _____

Sarah has _____ stickers left.

Name _____

1. Which number sentence does the picture show?

24

Ⓐ $14 - 10 = 4$

Ⓑ $36 - 14 = 22$

Ⓒ $22 + 10 = 32$

Ⓓ $14 + 10 = 24$

2. George has 31 cherries. Rose gives him 20 more cherrie
How many cherries does George have now?
Which number sentence can you use to solve the proble

Ⓐ $31 + 20 = 51$

Ⓑ $31 + 10 = 41$

Ⓒ $31 - 20 = 11$

Ⓓ $31 - 20 = 11$

3. Draw a picture. Write a number sentence.
Then solve the problem.

Carla has 25 orange stickers.
She has 20 purple stickers.
How many stickers does Carla have in all?

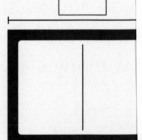

Tens One

____ 〇 ____ = ____

_____ stickers

Name _____

1. Clarissa blew up 67 balloons
for a party.
30 balloons popped.
How many balloons does
Clarissa have now?

1	2	3	4	5	6	7	8	9	10
11	12	13	14	15	16	17	18	19	20
21	22	23	24	25	26	27	28	29	30
31	32	33	34	35	36	37	38	39	40
41	42	43	44	45	46	47	48	49	50
51	52	53	54	55	56	57	58	59	60
61	62	63	64	65	66	67	68	69	70
71	72	73	74	75	76	77	78	79	80
81	82	83	84	85	86	87	88	89	90
91	92	93	94	95	96	97	98	99	100

Ⓐ 97

Ⓑ 64

Ⓒ 47

Ⓓ 37

2. Pedro brought 47 crackers for
the class party.
The class ate 40 crackers.
Which number sentence shows
how many crackers are left?

Ⓐ $47 - 40 = 7$

Ⓑ $47 - 37 = 10$

Ⓒ $47 - 4 = 43$

Ⓓ $47 + 40 = 87$

3. Pick and circle a number on
the hundred chart that is greater
than 40 and less than 100.
Subtract 30 from your number.
Complete the subtraction sentence.

_____ $- 30 =$ _____

Name _____

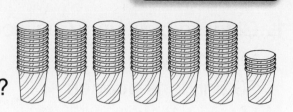

1. There are 64 dirty cups.
Audrey washes 20 cups.
How many cups are left to wash?

(A)　44

(B)　54

(C)　84

(D)　94

2. Gloria has 55 tickets for the play.
She sells 30 tickets.
Which number sentence shows
how many tickets Gloria has left?

(A)　$55 + 30 = 85$

(B)　$55 + 3 = 58$

(C)　$55 - 3 = 52$

(D)　$55 - 30 = 25$

3. Pick a number greater than 65
and less than 90.
Subtract 20, 30, or 40 from
your number.

Write a number sentence.

_____ − _____ = _____

Name _____

Subtract. Use mental math or ten-frame cards.

1. 56 − 20 = _____

Ⓐ 26

Ⓑ 36

Ⓒ 46

Ⓓ 56

2. 72 − 40 = _____

Ⓐ 32

Ⓑ 52

Ⓒ 62

Ⓓ 72

3. Writing in Math Choose a number from this list:
29, 73, 32, 81, 63, 54, 28.

Write the number in the box. Subtract 20.

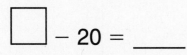 − 20 = _____

Tell what happens to the tens digit and the ones digit when you subtract.

_____

_____

Name _____

1. Which needs regrouping to subtract?

Ⓐ   12 − 5

Ⓑ   46 − 6

Ⓒ   18 − 2

Ⓓ   47 − 3

2. Herb needs to sell 32 tickets for the school carnival. He has sold 7 tickets so far. How many tickets does Herb have left to sell?

Tens	Ones

Ⓐ   39

Ⓑ   27

Ⓒ   25

Ⓓ   15

3. Write a subtraction sentence that uses regrouping. Draw a picture to solve it.

_____ − _____ = _____

Tens	Ones

1. Which number sentence shows the problem below?
A store has 50 tomatoes.
They sell 20 tomatoes.
How many tomatoes are left?

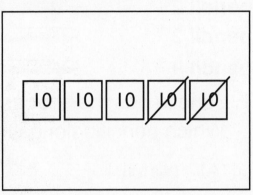

(A) $50 + 20 = 70$

(B) $50 + 30 = 80$

(C) $50 - 20 = 30$

(D) $50 - 30 = 20$

2. Jane has 40 stickers.
She gives her brother 10 stickers.
How many stickers does Jane have left?

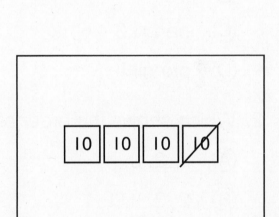

(A) 20 stickers

(B) 30 stickers

(C) 40 stickers

(D) 50 stickers

3. Draw a picture and write a number sentence to show the problem.
Then solve the problem.

Emily draws 50 stars.
Then she draws 20 hearts.
How many more stars than hearts did she draw?

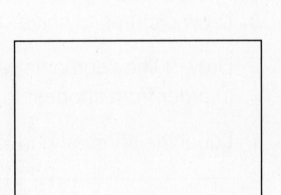

_____ − _____ = _____

Name _____

pencil 1

pencil 2

pencil 3

pencil 4

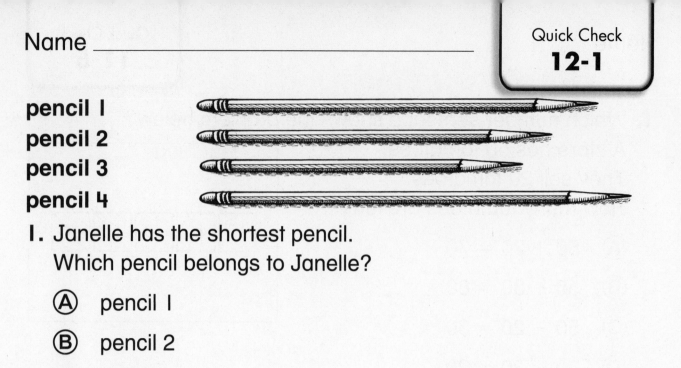

1. Janelle has the shortest pencil.
Which pencil belongs to Janelle?

Ⓐ pencil 1

Ⓑ pencil 2

Ⓒ pencil 3

Ⓓ pencil 4

2. Which shows the order of the pencils from longest to shortest?

Ⓐ 1, 2, 3, 4

Ⓑ 2, 3, 4, 1

Ⓒ 4, 1, 2, 3

Ⓓ 4, 3, 2, 1

3. Draw pictures to solve. Then write the labels.

Draw 4 line segments with different lengths
in order from shortest to longest.

Label the shortest and longest lines.

Name _____

Indirect Measurement

I. Choose the object that is shortest. Use the black string to help.

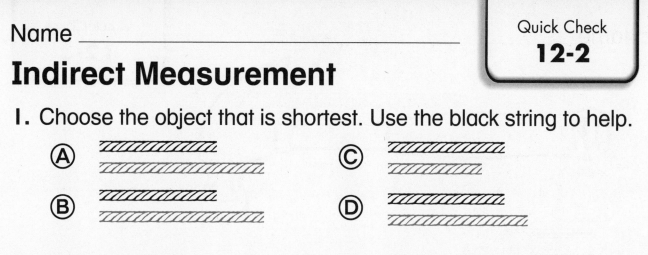

Ⓐ   Ⓒ

Ⓑ   Ⓓ

2. Which rectangle on the right is the tallest? Use the gray rectangle to help.

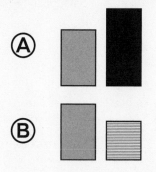

Ⓐ   Ⓒ

Ⓑ   Ⓓ

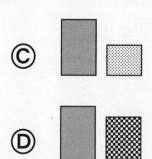

3. Find these objects in your classroom.
Compare the lengths of objects using a piece of yarn.
Circle the longest object. Mark an X on the shortest object.
Use words, objects, or pictures to tell how you know.

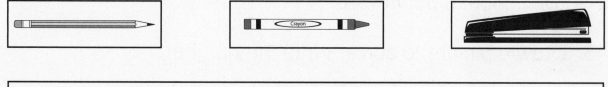

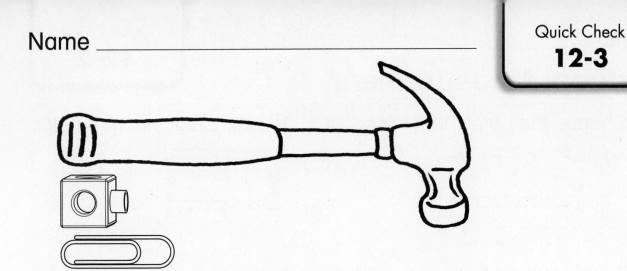

1. About how many cubes long is the hammer?

   (A) about 12 cubes

   (B) about 10 cubes

   (C) about 6 cubes

   (D) about 3 cubes

2. About how many paper clips long is the hammer?

   (A) about 1 paper clip

   (B) about 2 paper clips

   (C) about 3 paper clips

   (D) about 6 paper clips

3. Draw a picture to solve. Write the number.

   Clara's pencil is about 3 paper clips long.
   About how many cubes long is Clara's pencil? _____ cubes

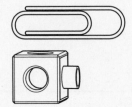

Name _____

1. Roberto's book is 9 cubes tall.
Lucy's book is 14 cubes tall.
Sophia's book is the tallest.
How tall might Sophia's book be?

Ⓐ 8 cubes

Ⓑ 12 cubes

Ⓒ 14 cubes

Ⓓ 16 cubes

2. Which object is the longest?

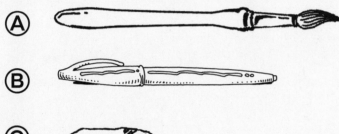

Ⓐ

Ⓑ

Ⓒ

Ⓓ

3. Draw these objects in order
from tallest to shortest.

1. About how many cubes long
is the paintbrush?

Ⓐ   about 3 cubes

Ⓑ   about 4 cubes

Ⓒ   about 6 cubes

Ⓓ   about 7 cubes

2. Which do you need the fewest of
to measure the paintbrush?

Ⓐ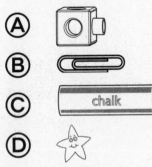

Ⓑ

Ⓒ   chalk

Ⓓ

3. Draw 2 different size paper clips below the feather.
Use each paper clip to estimate the length of the feather.
Write the numbers. Circle your answer.

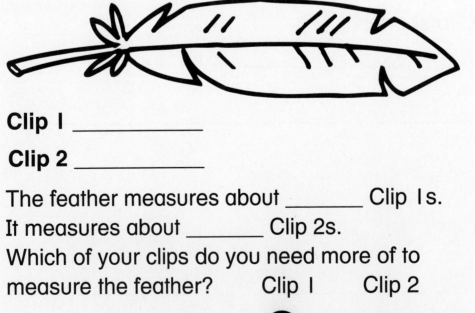

Clip 1 _____

Clip 2 _____

The feather measures about _____ Clip 1s.
It measures about _____ Clip 2s.
Which of your clips do you need more of to
measure the feather?   Clip 1   Clip 2

I. About how long is the crayon?

Ⓐ   0 cubes

Ⓑ   3 cubes

Ⓒ   5 cubes

Ⓓ   10 cubes

2. Vanessa plays the clarinet in the school band. Which is a good estimate for the length of Vanessa's clarinet?

Ⓐ   8 straws

Ⓑ   2 straws

Ⓒ   6 cubes

Ⓓ   2 cubes

3. Draw a caterpillar. Measure your caterpillar in cubes. Write its length.

The caterpillar is about _____ cubes long.

1. Which time does the clock show?

   Ⓐ   12 o'clock

   Ⓑ   7 o'clock

   Ⓒ   6 o'clock

   Ⓓ   5 o'clock

2. Which time is in between?

   Ⓐ   11 o'clock

   Ⓑ   12 o'clock

   Ⓒ   1 o'clock

   Ⓓ   2 o'clock

3. Use words or pictures.
Tell about 2 things you like to do at school.
Draw hands on the clock faces to show the times.

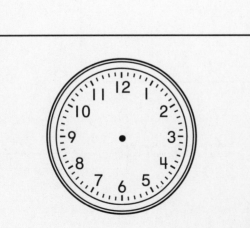

1. Which shows the same time as the clock face?

Ⓐ 10:00

Ⓑ 11:00

Ⓒ 12:00

Ⓓ 1:00

2. Which time is missing?

12:00, 11:00, _____, 9:00, 8:00

Ⓐ 10:00

Ⓑ 9:00

Ⓒ 8:00

Ⓓ 7:00

3. Use words or pictures.
Tell about something
you do after school.
Show the time in
2 different ways.

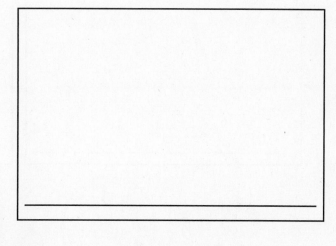

I. Which shows the same time
as the clock face?

Ⓐ 8:30

Ⓑ 8:00

Ⓒ 7:30

Ⓓ 7:00

2. Which tells the time it will be
in 30 minutes?

Ⓐ 11:30

Ⓑ 12:00

Ⓒ 1:00

Ⓓ 1:30

3. Use words or pictures.
Tell about something you do a half hour before bedtime.

Draw the clock hands. Write the time.

Go to bed.

9:00

Name _____

Movie Schedule	
Time	**Movie**
12:30	*The Happy Mouse*
2:30	*Katie the Detective*
3:00	*Billy's Adventure*
4:00	*The Mystery Carpet*

1. Which movie starts at 2:30?

Ⓐ *The Happy Mouse*

Ⓑ *Katie the Detective*

Ⓒ *Billy's Adventure*

Ⓓ *The Mystery Carpet*

2. What time does *Billy's Adventure* start?

Ⓐ 4:00

Ⓑ 3:00

Ⓒ 2:30

Ⓓ 12:30

3. Fill in the times for your schedule.
Answer the question.

My Afternoon at School	
Time	**Activity**
_____	Lunch begins
_____	Lunch ends
_____	Recess
_____	School day ends

How long is your lunch period? _____ minutes

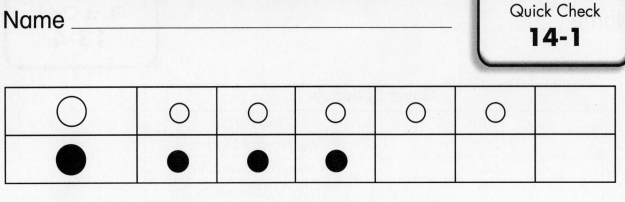

1. How many counters do not have a partner?

(A) 3

(B) 2

(C) 1

(D) 0

2. Which does the graph show?

(A) There are more black counters.

(B) There are 5 black counters.

(C) There are 2 fewer black counters.

(D) There are 3 more white counters.

3. Writing in Math Write a question about the graph below. Then write the answer.

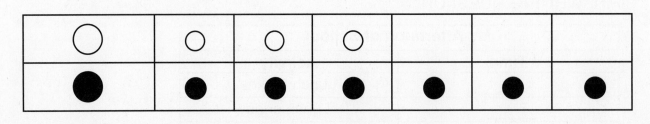

Question: _____

Answer: _____

Favorite Animals

Lion						
Elephant						
Tiger						
Monkey						

1. How many more children chose Tigers than Elephants?

Ⓐ 1

Ⓑ 2

Ⓒ 3

Ⓓ 4

2. Which animals were chosen by the same number of children?

Ⓐ Lion and Elephant

Ⓑ Tiger and Lion

Ⓒ Monkey and Tiger

Ⓓ Elephant and Tiger

3. Writing in Math Write a question about the graph below. Then write the answer.

Favorite Ways to Skate

Roller skate						
Ice skate						
Skateboard						

Question: _____

Answer: _____

Name _____

1. Which pet is the favorite?

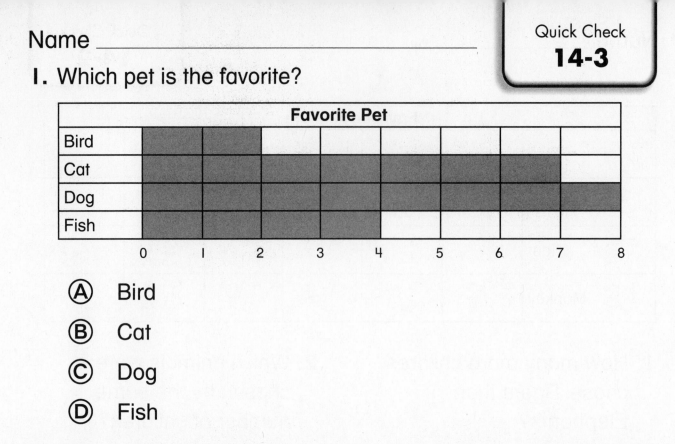

Favorite Pet

	0	1	2	3	4	5	6	7	8
Bird									
Cat									
Dog									
Fish									

Ⓐ Bird

Ⓑ Cat

Ⓒ Dog

Ⓓ Fish

2. How many more children chose Fish than Bird as a favorite pet?

Ⓐ 4

Ⓑ 3

Ⓒ 2

Ⓓ 1

3. Writing in Math Write a question about the graph below. Then write the answer.

Favorite Things to Read About

	0	1	2	3	4	5	6	7	8
Animals									
People									
Places									

Question: _____

Answer: _____

Terrell spun the spinner 20 times.
He made a tally mark for each spin.

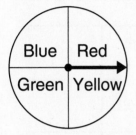

Spinner Colors	
Blue	~~||||~~ ||
Red	|||
Green	~~||||~~	
Yellow	||||

I. How many more times did the spinner land on green than yellow?

Ⓐ I

Ⓑ 2

Ⓒ 3

Ⓓ 4

2. Which color did Terrell spin most often?

Ⓐ Blue

Ⓑ Red

Ⓒ Green

Ⓓ Yellow

3. Color the stickers.
Make the tallies.
Write the numbers.

Camille has some red, blue,
and green stickers.
She has at least 5 of each color.

Color	Tally	Total
Red		
Blue		
Green		

Name _____

Bella uses cubes to make a graph that shows
the pencils she has.

Bella's Pencils						
⬛ Red	⬛	⬛	⬛	⬛	⬛	⬛
⬛ Blue	⬛	⬛	⬛	⬛	⬛	
⬛ Green	⬛	⬛				

1. Which shows tallies for Bella's blue pencils?

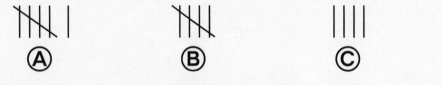

 Ⓐ   Ⓑ   Ⓒ   Ⓓ

2. Bella buys 3 more green pencils.
How many green pencils does she have now?

 2   4   5   6
 Ⓐ   Ⓑ   Ⓒ   Ⓓ

3. Make the tally chart.
Then use your tally chart
to make a graph.

Ben has 7 cubes.
Some are orange and
some are yellow.

Ben's Cubes – Tally Chart		
Orange		
Yellow		

Ben's Cubes – Real Graph					
Orange					
Yellow					

Name _____

Favorite Insects

 Butterfly						
Beetle						
Cricket						

1. How many more children voted for the Beetle rather than the Cricket?

   6   4   3   2

  Ⓐ   Ⓑ   Ⓒ   Ⓓ

2. Which shows the insects in order from least to most favorite?

  Ⓐ   Butterfly, Beetle, Cricket

  Ⓑ   Beetle, Butterfly, Cricket

  Ⓒ   Cricket, Beetle, Butterfly

  Ⓓ   Cricket, Butterfly, Beetle

3. Make the tally chart.
Use the tally chart to make
a picture graph.

Madison has 9 pieces of fruit in all.
She has more than 3 bananas.
The rest are apples.

Madison's Fruit

Apples		
Bananas		

Madison's Fruit

Apples					
Bananas					

Name _____

Judi's class made a bar graph to show their favorite toys.

1. How many fewer Kites were chosen than Trains?

    Ⓐ 4

    Ⓑ 3

    Ⓒ 2

    Ⓓ I

2. Which is the least favorite toy?

    Ⓐ Blocks

    Ⓑ Balls

    Ⓒ Trains

    Ⓓ Kites

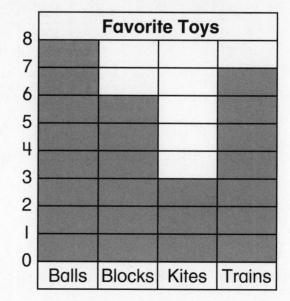

Favorite Toys — bar graph with categories Balls, Blocks, Kites, Trains

3. Use the clues to make a graph. Write the names in order from greatest to least number of books.

Eli has 6 books.
Abe has fewer books than Eli.
Nell has more books than Abe.
She has fewer than Eli.

Number of Books — blank graph

_____   _____   _____
greatest   least

Name _____

1. Which plane shape is
a triangle?

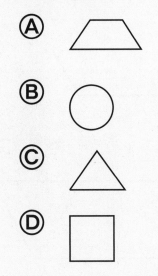

Ⓐ

Ⓑ

Ⓒ

Ⓓ

2. Cary drew a plane shape
that looks like a counter.
It looks like a CD.
Which plane shape did
Cary draw?

Ⓐ   square

Ⓑ   triangle

Ⓒ   circle

Ⓓ   rectangle

3. Draw a rectangle. Then draw
an everyday object that
has this shape.

Name _____

1. How many ▱ do you need to make this shape?

Ⓐ 2

Ⓑ 3

Ⓒ 4

Ⓓ 6

2. How many △ do you need to make this shape?

Ⓐ 8

Ⓑ 6

Ⓒ 5

Ⓓ 4

3. How many ways can you make this shape using pattern blocks?

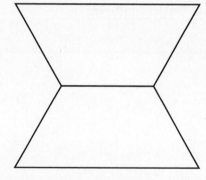

Shapes I Used	⬓	▱	△
Way 1			
Way 2			
Way 3			
Way 4			
Way 5			

Name _____

1. Which plane shape has more than
5 straight sides?

Ⓐ ○

Ⓑ △

Ⓒ ⬭ (trapezoid)

Ⓓ ⬡

2. How many corners does
this plane shape have?

Ⓐ 0

Ⓑ 3

Ⓒ 4

Ⓓ 5

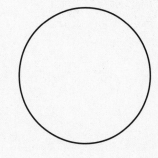

3. Writing in Math
Draw some shapes.
Then sort them into
2 groups.
Write your sorting rule.

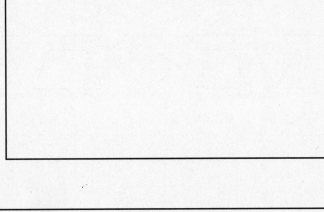

Sorting rule: _____

1. How many of each shape
are used to make this flower?

Ⓐ 2 ⬡ 1 ▱ 6 △

Ⓑ 1 ⬡ 2 ▱ 6 △

Ⓒ 1 ⬡ 6 ▱ 2 △

Ⓓ 3 ⬡ 2 ▱ 6 △

2. Tasha is making a three-leaf clover.
Which shape is missing from the picture?

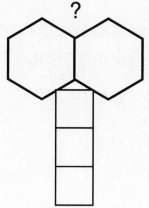

Ⓐ ⬡

Ⓑ ☐

Ⓒ △

Ⓓ ▱

3. Use pattern blocks to make a picture.
You must use more than 4 blocks.
Write how many of each shape you use.

I. How many triangle pattern blocks
do you need to make ?

Ⓐ 3

Ⓑ 2

Ⓒ I

Ⓓ 0

2. Which 2 pattern blocks could
you use to make this shape?

Ⓐ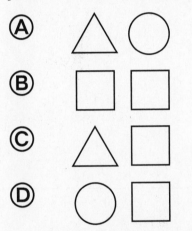

Ⓑ

Ⓒ

Ⓓ

3. Draw 2 plane shapes that
you can use to make a new
shape. Then draw your new
plane shape.

1. Which solid figure has the same shape as the ice cream cone?

Ⓐ rectangular prism

Ⓑ cone

Ⓒ sphere

Ⓓ cube

2. Gina puts a solid figure on the table.
The solid figure rolls.
Which solid figure is **not** on the table?

Ⓐ sphere

Ⓑ cone

Ⓒ cylinder

Ⓓ cube

3. Writing in Math Write a riddle about an everyday object that is like a solid figure.
Draw the solid figure that is most like the object.

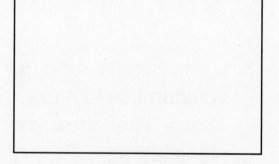

Riddle: _____

_____

My solid figure is a _____ .

Name _____

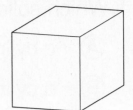

1. Which is true about the cube?

    Ⓐ   It has 6 flat surfaces and 6 vertices.

    Ⓑ   It has 6 flat surfaces and 8 vertices.

    Ⓒ   It has 4 flat surfaces and 6 vertices.

    Ⓓ   It has 4 flat surfaces and 4 vertices.

2. Which solid figure has 2 flat surfaces
   and 0 vertices?

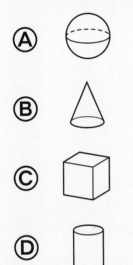

    Ⓐ

    Ⓑ

    Ⓒ

    Ⓓ

3. **Writing in Math** Write 4 clues
   about a solid figure.
   Draw the figure.

_____

_____

_____

_____

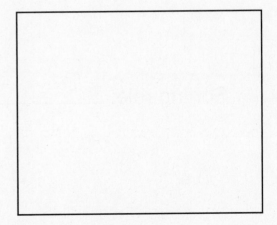

Name _____

1. Which solid figures have fewer than 3 flat surfaces?

Ⓐ a cylinder and a cube

Ⓑ a cylinder and a cone

Ⓒ a rectangular prism and a cube

Ⓓ a sphere and a cube

2. Which sorting rule describes these 2 solid figures?

Ⓐ The solid figures roll.

Ⓑ The solid figures have 6 vertices.

Ⓒ The solid figures have 8 vertices.

Ⓓ The solid figures have 8 flat surfaces.

3. **Writing in Math**
   Draw some solid figures.
   Then sort them into
   2 groups.
   Write your sorting rule.

Sorting rule: _____.

Name _____

1. Which 2 solid figures make the clown?

Ⓐ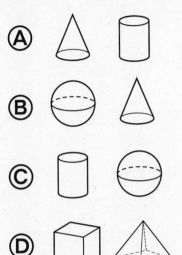

Ⓑ

Ⓒ

Ⓓ

2. Ben made an object using these solid shapes. Which object did Ben make?

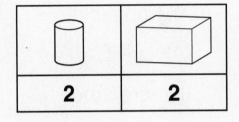

2	2

Ⓐ

Ⓑ

Ⓒ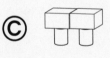

Ⓓ

3. **Writing in Math** Lauren made a building with solid shapes.
Name the shapes she used.
Tell how many of each shape she used.

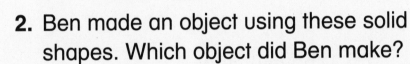

_____

_____

Name _____

Which shows something that is always
true of these shapes?

1. All of these shapes are cones.
   All cones:

   Ⓐ have 1 flat surface   Ⓒ are gray

   Ⓑ are small   Ⓓ have a flat bottom

2. All of these shapes are
   trapezoids.
   All trapezoids:

   Ⓐ are big   Ⓒ have 4 sides

   Ⓑ are small   Ⓓ are white

3. **Writing in Math**
   Think of a plane shape.
   Write two things that are always true about
   your plane shape.
   Then draw a picture of your shape.

   _____

   _____

Name _____

1. Terry drew a line to make 2 equal parts.
Which picture shows what Terry drew?

Ⓐ

Ⓑ

Ⓒ

Ⓓ

2. How many equal parts
are shown in the picture?

Ⓐ 6

Ⓑ 4

Ⓒ 3

Ⓓ 0

3. Draw straight lines to divide
each shape into 2 or 4 equal parts.

Then write the number of equal parts
for each shape.

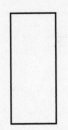  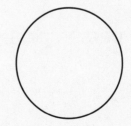

_____   _____   _____

Name _____

1. Which does the picture show?

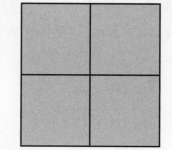

   Ⓐ   1 out of 2 equal parts

   Ⓑ   2 out of 4 equal parts

   Ⓒ   3 out of 4 equal parts

   Ⓓ   4 out of 4 equal parts

2. Which tells how much
of the rectangle is shaded?

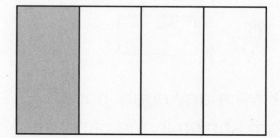

   Ⓐ   1 out of 4 equal parts

   Ⓑ   1 out of 3 equal parts

   Ⓒ   1 out of 2 equal parts

   Ⓓ   3 out of 4 equal parts

3. Draw a picture to solve.
Write the number.

Julia and 3 friends share
the bagel.
How many equal parts does
each person get?
Draw a picture to solve.

Each person gets _____ out of _____ equal parts.

1. Which figure has half shaded?

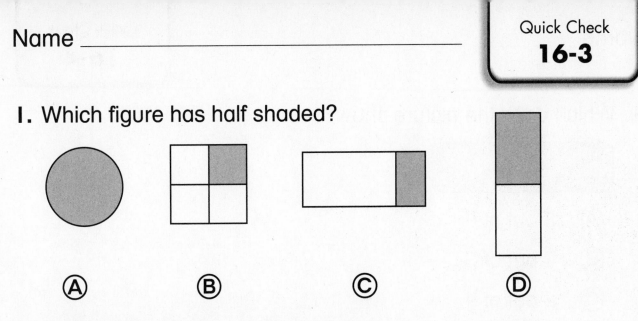

Ⓐ   Ⓑ   Ⓒ   Ⓓ

2. Which best describes the figure?

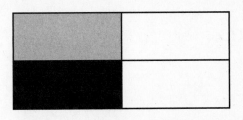

Ⓐ   A fourth of the rectangle is white.

Ⓑ   A fourth of the rectangle is black.

Ⓒ   A half of the rectangle is gray.

Ⓓ   A half of the rectangle is black.

3. Leah has the ribbon below. She wants to give half to her sister. Use words or pictures to tell where Leah should cut the ribbon. Then show the amount Leah's sister will get.

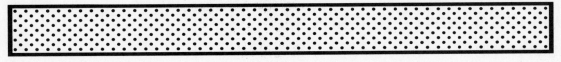

Name _____

1. Which does the picture show?

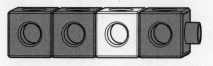

Ⓐ   3 out of 4

Ⓑ   2 out of 3

Ⓒ   2 out of 4

Ⓓ   1 out of 4

2. Deb draws a shape with 4 equal parts.
2 out of 4 parts have dots.
The rest are all stripes.

Which shows Deb's shape?

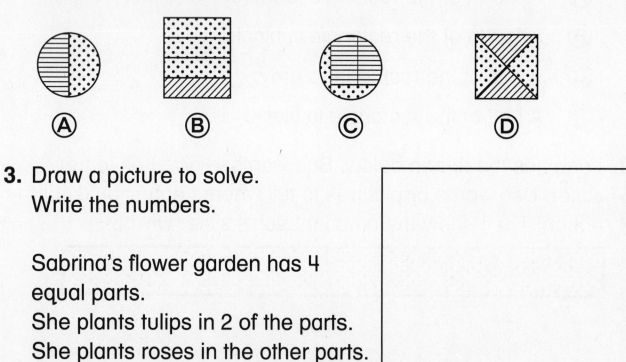

Ⓐ   Ⓑ   Ⓒ   Ⓓ

3. Draw a picture to solve.
Write the numbers.

Sabrina's flower garden has 4
equal parts.
She plants tulips in 2 of the parts.
She plants roses in the other parts.
What part of the garden has tulips?

_____ out of _____ parts have tulips.

Name _____

Mark the best answer.

1. Which number does the picture show?

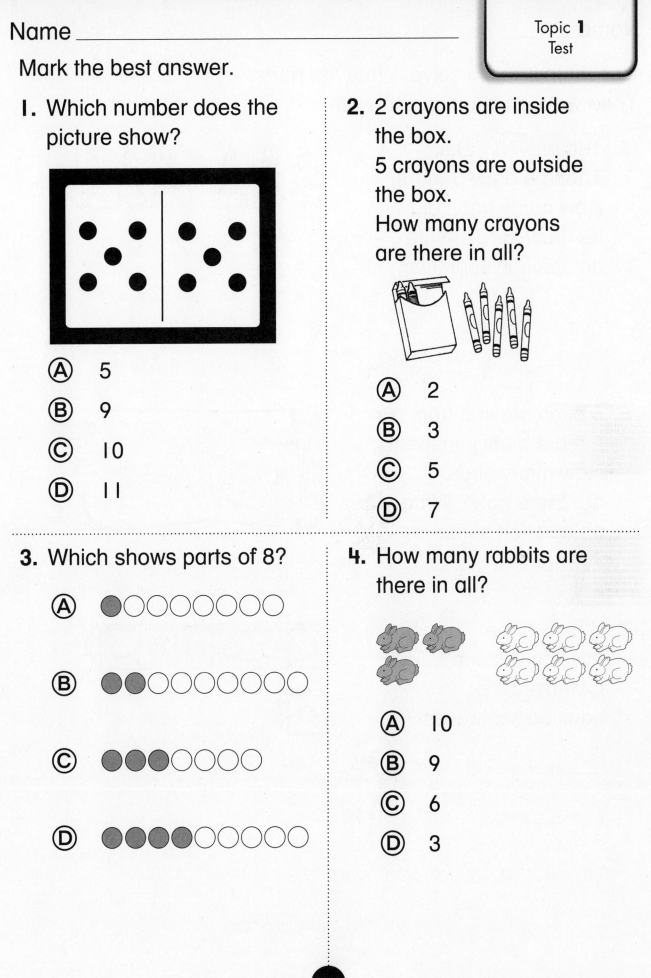

Ⓐ 5

Ⓑ 9

Ⓒ 10

Ⓓ 11

2. 2 crayons are inside the box.
5 crayons are outside the box.
How many crayons are there in all?

Ⓐ 2

Ⓑ 3

Ⓒ 5

Ⓓ 7

3. Which shows parts of 8?

Ⓐ ●○○○○○○○

Ⓑ ●●○○○○○○

Ⓒ ●●●○○○○

Ⓓ ●●●●○○○○

4. How many rabbits are there in all?

Ⓐ 10

Ⓑ 9

Ⓒ 6

Ⓓ 3

Name _____

Use the picture to solve. Write the parts.
Then write an addition sentence.

5. Ted drew 3 trees.
Then he drew 3 more.
How many trees did
he draw in all? Write
an addition sentence.

___ + ___

___ + ___ = ___

6. 6 birds are in a tree.
2 more birds join them.
How many birds
are there now? Write
an addition sentence.

___ + ___ = ___

7. Which is the
missing addend?
Complete the
addition sentences.

___ + 1 = 7

1 + ___ = 7

Name _____

Mark the best answer.

Find the missing part for exercises 1 and 2.

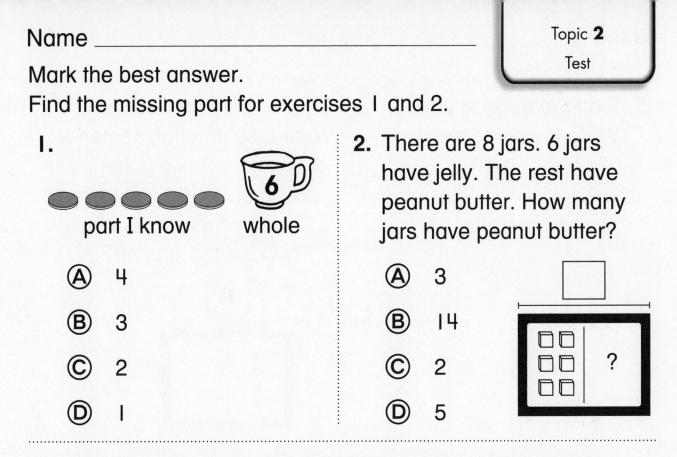

1.

part I know   whole

Ⓐ 4

Ⓑ 3

Ⓒ 2

Ⓓ 1

2. There are 8 jars. 6 jars have jelly. The rest have peanut butter. How many jars have peanut butter?

Ⓐ 3

Ⓑ 14

Ⓒ 2

Ⓓ 5

3. Use cubes to solve. Choose the number sentence that shows the story.

Faiza has 3 purses. She gives 2 away as gifts. How many purses does Faiza have left?

$3 - 2 = 1$ $3 + 2 = 5$ $5 - 2 = 3$ $5 - 3 = 2$

Ⓐ   Ⓑ   Ⓒ   Ⓓ

4. Roberto ate 10 crackers. Carrie ate 5 crackers. How many more crackers did Roberto eat than Carrie?

$10 + 5 = 15$ $15 - 5 = 10$ $10 - 5 = 5$ $5 + 5 = 10$

Ⓐ   Ⓑ   Ⓒ   Ⓓ

Name _____

5. Find the missing part. Write the numbers.

9

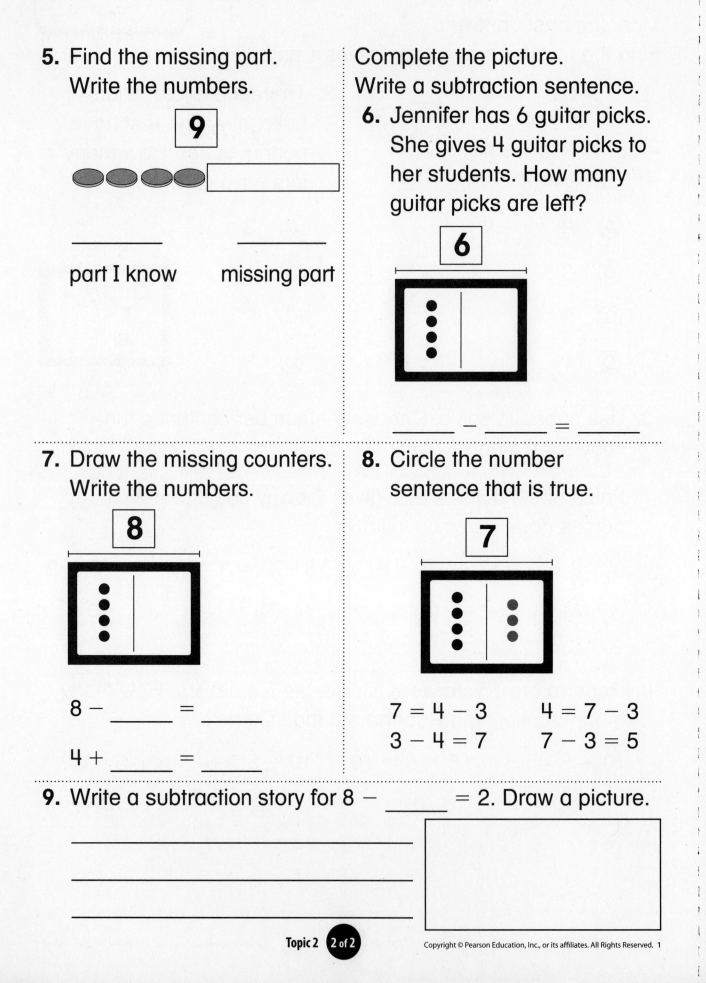

_____   _____
part I know   missing part

Complete the picture. Write a subtraction sentence.

6. Jennifer has 6 guitar picks. She gives 4 guitar picks to her students. How many guitar picks are left?

6

_____ – _____ = _____

7. Draw the missing counters. Write the numbers.

8

8 – _____ = _____

4 + _____ = _____

8. Circle the number sentence that is true.

7

$7 = 4 - 3$ $4 = 7 - 3$
$3 - 4 = 7$ $7 - 3 = 5$

9. Write a subtraction story for 8 – _____ = 2. Draw a picture.

_____

_____

_____

Mark the best answer.

I. Ava drew 4 counters in a ten-frame. How many more counters does Ava need to draw to make 10?

Ⓐ 10

Ⓑ 7

Ⓒ 6

Ⓓ 5

2. Which sentence describes the ten-frame?

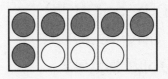

Ⓐ 5 and 3 is 9.

Ⓑ 2 away from 10 is 9.

Ⓒ 6 and 3 is 9.

Ⓓ 3 away from 10 is 9.

3. Which number does the ten-frame show?

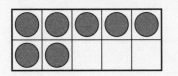

Ⓐ 3

Ⓑ 7

Ⓒ 8

Ⓓ 10

4. Which is a way to make 10?

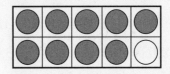

Ⓐ 10 is 1 and 8.

Ⓑ 10 is 1 and 7.

Ⓒ 10 is 9 and 1.

Ⓓ 10 is 9 and 2.

Name _____

Mark the best answer.

5. Marni and Della have
10 counters altogether.
Marni has 8 counters.
How many counters
does Della have?

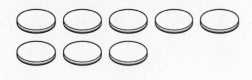

_____ counters

6. Draw the missing part.
Write the number.

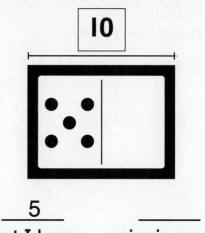

5	_____
part I know	missing part

7. Blair buys 3 shirts.
The store sells blue shirts
and yellow shirts.
If Blair buys 2 blue shirts,
how many yellow shirts
does she buy? Write the
missing number in the table.

Blue	Yellow
3	0
2	
1	2
0	3

Name _____

Mark the best answer.

1. Kevin paints 8 toy boats. Sam paints 0 more toy boats than Kevin. Which tells how many boats Sam painted?

Ⓐ 8 + 0 = 8

Ⓑ 7 + 0 = 7

Ⓒ 4 + 2 = 6

Ⓓ 0 + 0 = 0

2. Which sentences with 5 and 10 tell about the model?

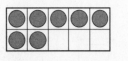

Ⓐ 5 + 2 = 7
    7 + 3 = 10

Ⓑ 5 + 2 = 7
    6 + 4 = 10

Ⓒ 3 + 2 = 5
    5 + 2 = 7

Ⓓ 5 + 0 = 5
    2 + 0 = 2

3. 4 + 5 is _____

Ⓐ 5 + 6 and 1 more

Ⓑ 5 + 5 and 1 more

Ⓒ 4 + 4 and 1 more

Ⓓ 3 + 3 and 1 more

4. Which number sentence helps you add 9 + 3?

Ⓐ 10 + 4 = 14

Ⓑ 10 + 3 = 13

Ⓒ 10 + 2 = 12

Ⓓ 10 + 1 = 11

Name _____

Mark the best answer.

5. Complete the addition fact. Then use the addition fact to subtract.

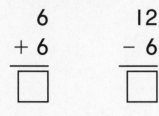

$$6 + 6 = \square$$

$$12 - 6 = \square$$

6. Which number completes the sentences?

____ less than 7 is 6.

$$7 - \_\_\_ = 6$$

7. Tracey makes 8 bracelets. She gives 6 to her friends. How many bracelets does Tracey have left?

Write an addition sentence and a subtraction sentence.

____ + ____ = ____

____ − ____ = ____

8. Akeem needs to wrap 11 presents. He wraps 7 presents. How many more presents does Akeem need to wrap?

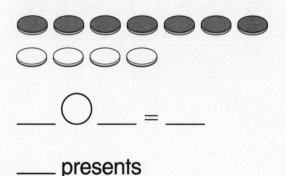

____ ◯ ____ = ____

____ presents

9. Draw a picture and write a subtraction sentence to solve. There were 9 children on the bus. 3 children got off the bus. How many children were left on the bus?

____ − ____ = ____ children

Name _____

Solve the problems below.

1.
$$8$$
$$+\ 8$$
⟨A⟩ 14
⟨B⟩ 15
⟨C⟩ 16
⟨D⟩ 17

2.
$$6$$
$$+\ 7$$
⟨A⟩ 11
⟨B⟩ 12
⟨C⟩ 13
⟨D⟩ 14

3.
$$10$$
$$+\ 8$$
⟨A⟩ 20
⟨B⟩ 18
⟨C⟩ 17
⟨D⟩ 15

4.
$$5$$
$$6$$
$$+\ 9$$
⟨A⟩ 17
⟨B⟩ 18
⟨C⟩ 19
⟨D⟩ 20

5. Which two number sentences help you solve the problem?

Wen buys 12 eggs.
9 eggs break.
How many eggs are left?

Then Wen buys 5 more eggs.
How many eggs are there?

⟨A⟩ $12 - 9 = 3$ and $5 - 3 = 2$

⟨B⟩ $9 + 3 = 12$ and $12 - 5 = 7$

⟨C⟩ $12 - 9 = 3$ and $3 + 5 = 8$

⟨D⟩ $9 + 5 = 14$ and $14 - 2 = 12$

Name _____

Draw the missing counters.
Then write the sums.

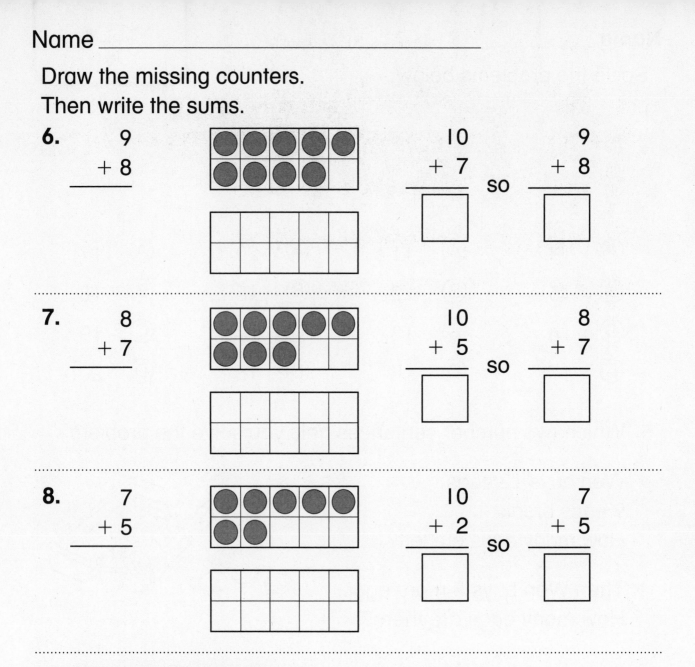

6.　　9
　　　+ 8
　　　_____

10
+ 7
_____
☐

so

9
+ 8
_____
☐

7.　　8
　　　+ 7
　　　_____

10
+ 5
_____
☐

so

8
+ 7
_____
☐

8.　　7
　　　+ 5
　　　_____

10
+ 2
_____
☐

so

7
+ 5
_____
☐

9. Eli painted 6 pictures.

Marly painted 8 pictures.

Their friend Dara painted 5 more pictures.

How many pictures did the three children paint in all?

_____ + _____ + _____ = _____

_____ pictures

Name _____

Mark the best answer.

1. Which is a related subtraction fact for $7 + 9 = 16$?

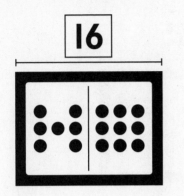

Ⓐ $9 - 7 = 2$

Ⓑ $16 - 9 = 7$

Ⓒ $8 + 8 = 16$

Ⓓ $20 - 10 = 10$

2. Find the missing fact from this fact family.

$6 + 8 = 14$
$14 - 8 = 6$
$14 - 6 = 8$

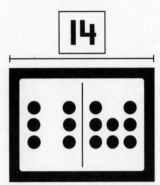

Ⓐ $8 - 6 = 2$

Ⓑ $8 + 6 = 14$

Ⓒ $14 - 5 = 9$

Ⓓ $8 - 2 = 6$

3. There are 16 dogs in the park.
Then 9 dogs leave.
How many dogs are left?
Make a 10 to solve.

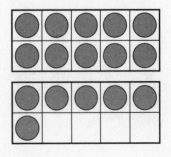

Ⓐ 5

Ⓑ 6

Ⓒ 7

Ⓓ 8

Name _____

4. Write the missing numbers for these related facts.

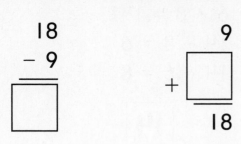

5. Complete the model. Then complete the number sentences.

15 − 6 = _____

6 + _____ = 15

6. Write a number sentence to match the picture.

_____ ◯ _____ = _____

Name _____

Mark the best answer.

1. Which number is 10 and 3 ones?

Ⓐ 3

Ⓑ 10

Ⓒ 13

Ⓓ 31

2. Bob has 17 pencils. Jane has 2 fewer pencils than Bob. How many pencils does Jane have?

Ⓐ 13

Ⓑ 15

Ⓒ 19

Ⓓ 20

3. Jennifer has 13 markers. Nita has 2 fewer markers than Jennifer. How many markers does Nita have?

Ⓐ 11

Ⓑ 12

Ⓒ 14

Ⓓ 16

4. Count by 10s to find the number.

Ⓐ 5

Ⓑ 10

Ⓒ 50

Ⓓ 100

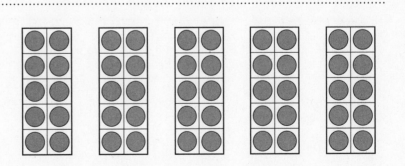

Name _____

Look at each part of the hundred chart.
Write the missing numbers.

5.

	57		59	
66		68		70

6.

		78
	87	
	97	

7. Find a pattern. Skip count.
How many fingers are
there in all?

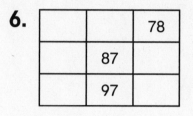

_____, _____, _____

There are _____ fingers in all.

8. Janet has 4 plants.
Each plant has 5 leaves.
How many leaves in all?

Plants	1	2	3	4
Leaves	5			

There are _____ leaves in all.

Mark the best answer.

1. __?__ is 1 group of 10 and 6 left over.

Ⓐ 6

Ⓑ 10

Ⓒ 16

Ⓓ 60

2. 28 is __?__ groups of 10 and 8 left over.

Ⓐ 2

Ⓑ 8

Ⓒ 20

Ⓓ 80

3. Count by 10s. Find how many. 7 tens is __?__.

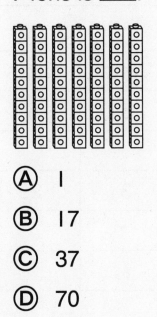

Ⓐ 1

Ⓑ 17

Ⓒ 37

Ⓓ 70

4. Count the tens and ones. Find the number.

Tens	Ones

Ⓐ 4

Ⓑ 6

Ⓒ 46

Ⓓ 64

Name _____

Mark the best answer.

5. Draw the tens and ones.
Then write the numbers.

Tens	Ones

_____ tens + _____ ones = _____

_____ + _____ = _____

....

6. Eliza made this model.
What number is she showing?

_____

_____ = _____ + _____

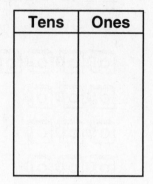

....

7. Kerry's list shows ways to make 55.
Complete Kerry's list.

Tens	Ones
5	5
3	25

Mark the best answer.

1. Jim has 13 cubes.
Li gives him 10
more cubes.
How many cubes
does Jim have now?

(A)   130

(B)   23

(C)   13

(D)   3

2. Which number completes
the section of the
hundred chart?

	62	
71	?	73
	82	

(A)   82

(B)   74

(C)   72

(D)   70

3. Which sentence
compares the cubes?

(A)   43 > 25

(B)   43 = 25

(C)   25 > 43

(D)   43 < 25

4. Which number is
missing?

45	46	47
55	56	57
65	?	67

(A)   77

(B)   68

(C)   66

(D)   56

5. Write the numbers that are 10 more and 10 less.

_____ 63 _____

10 less   10 more

6. Tom gets 3 number cards with the numbers 18, 30, and 22. Write the numbers in order from least to greatest.

_____ _____ _____

---

7. Write <, >, or = to make the sentences true.

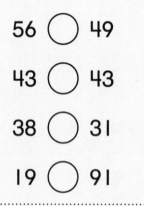

56 ◯ 49

43 ◯ 43

38 ◯ 31

19 ◯ 91

---

8. Complete the list to find the secret number.

| 42 | 70 | 50 | 60 | 37 | 40 |

I am greater than 39 but less than 55.

What number could I be?

_____

_____

_____

I am less than 50. You can say my name when you count by tens. What number am I?

_____

Name _____

Mark the best answer.

1. Add tens to complete the number sentence.
5 tens + 2 tens = ?

(A) 2

(B) 7

(C) 2 tens

(D) 7 tens

....

2. Use the part of a hundred chart to add.

51	52	53	54	55	56	57	58	59	60
61	62	63	64	65	66	67	68	69	70
71	72	73	74	75	76	77	78	79	80
81	82	83	84	85	86				

55 + 20 = ?

(A) 85

(B) 75

(C) 63

(D) 70

....

3. Look at the picture. Find the matching number sentence.

(A) 23 + 20 = 43

(B) 23 − 10 = 13

(C) 23 + 30 = 53

(D) 23 − 13 = 10

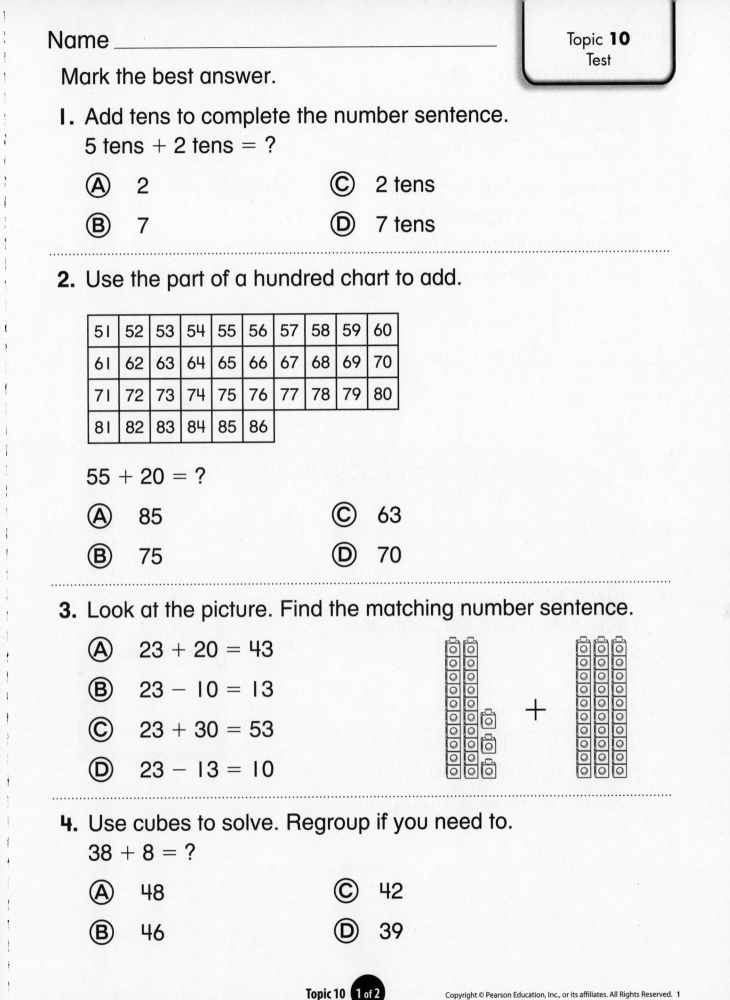

....

4. Use cubes to solve. Regroup if you need to.
38 + 8 = ?

(A) 48

(B) 46

(C) 42

(D) 39

Name _____

Use mental math to solve.

5. 5l + l0 = _____

....

6. There are 35 bananas and
l0 pears in a basket.
How many pieces of fruit
are there in the basket?

_____

....

7. 37 + l0 = _____

....

Write the missing numbers. Regroup if you need to.

8. 42 + 9 = _____   **9.** 53 + 6 = _____

....

l0. Draw a picture.
Then write a number sentence
to solve.

Stella buys l9 cookies.
Lucas buys 20 cookies.
How many cookies do
Lucas and Stella buy altogether?

_____ cookies   _____ + _____ = _____

Name _____

Mark your answers for
Exercises 1–3.

1. Use the hundred chart to subtract tens.

61	62	63	64	65	66	67	68	69	70
71	72	73	74	75	76	77	78	79	80
81	82	83	84	85	86	87	88	89	90

87 − 20 = _____

(A) 80   (C) 60

(B) 67   (D) 77

2. Use the cubes. Find the difference. Regroup if you need to.

66 − 9 = _____

(A) 50   (C) 57

(B) 55   (D) 69

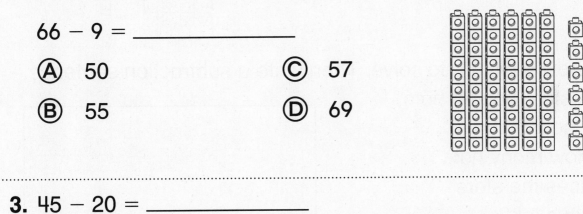

3. 45 − 20 = _____

(A) 65   (C) 40

(B) 55   (D) 25

Name _____

4. Look at the model.
Write the numbers to complete the number sentences.

_____ tens − _____ tens = _____ tens

_____ − _____ = _____

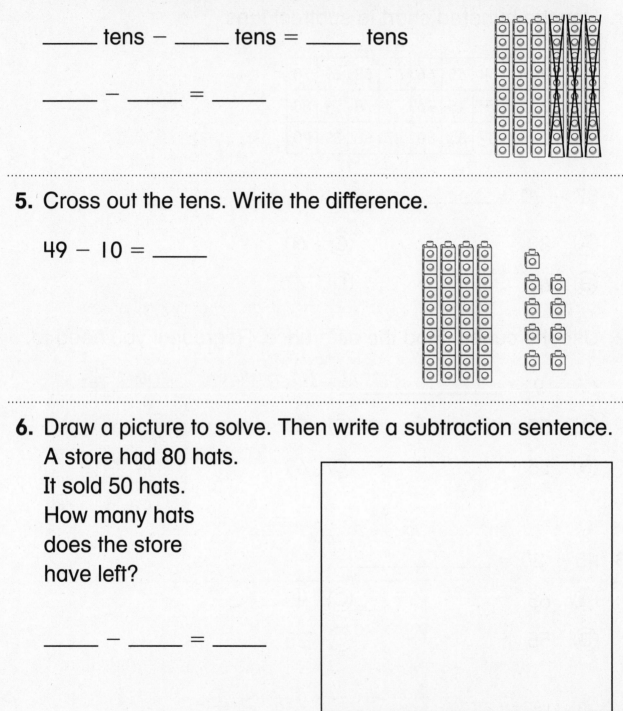

....

5. Cross out the tens. Write the difference.

49 − 10 = _____

....

6. Draw a picture to solve. Then write a subtraction sentence.
A store had 80 hats.
It sold 50 hats.
How many hats
does the store
have left?

_____ − _____ = _____

Name _____

I. Which list shows the items from longest to shortest?

    Ⓐ   screwdriver, screw, hammer

    Ⓑ   screw, hammer, screwdriver

    Ⓒ   screw, screwdriver, hammer

    Ⓓ   hammer, screwdriver, screw

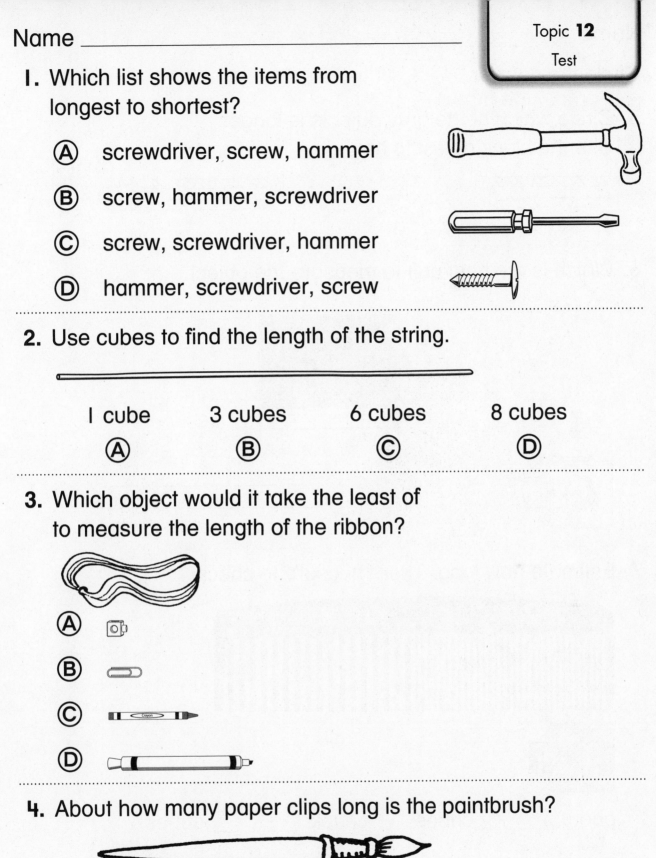

2. Use cubes to find the length of the string.

I cube	3 cubes	6 cubes	8 cubes
Ⓐ	Ⓑ	Ⓒ	Ⓓ

3. Which object would it take the least of to measure the length of the ribbon?

    Ⓐ

    Ⓑ

    Ⓒ

    Ⓓ

4. About how many paper clips long is the paintbrush?

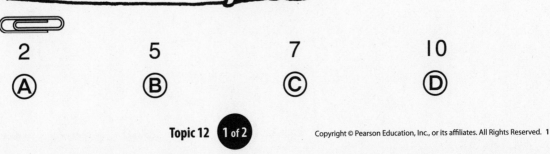

2	5	7	10
Ⓐ	Ⓑ	Ⓒ	Ⓓ

Name _____

Circle the answer.

5. Circle which of the gray objects is longer.
Use the black object to help.

---

6. Which is the best unit to measure the object.

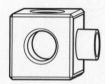

---

7. Estimate how long. Then measure to check.

about _____ cubes   check: _____ cubes

Name _____

Mark the best answer.

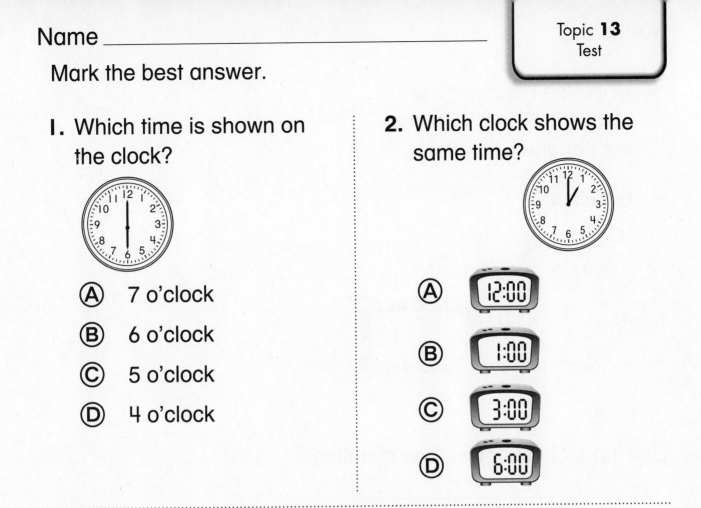

1. Which time is shown on the clock?

Ⓐ 7 o'clock

Ⓑ 6 o'clock

Ⓒ 5 o'clock

Ⓓ 4 o'clock

2. Which clock shows the same time?

Ⓐ 12:00

Ⓑ 1:00

Ⓒ 3:00

Ⓓ 6:00

3. Which clock shows the same time?

5:30

Ⓐ   Ⓑ   Ⓒ   Ⓓ

Name _____

4. Draw the hands on the clock face. Then write the time on the other clock.

6 o'clock

....

Use the table to answer the questions.

Birthday Party Schedule	
Time	**Activity**
11:00	Play Games
12:00	Eat Lunch
12:30	Balloon Animals
1:00	Open Presents

5. When does Play Games begin?

_____

....

6. Which activity is just before Open Presents?

_____

   1

Name _____

1. Lucas made a graph to show his cubes. Which sentence tells about his cubes?

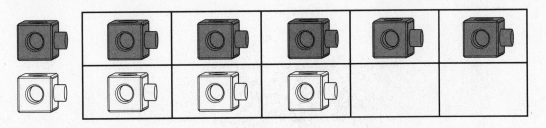

Ⓐ Lucas has 2 more gray cubes than white cubes.

Ⓑ Lucas has more white cubes than gray cubes.

Ⓒ Lucas has 5 cubes in all.

Ⓓ Lucas has 5 gray cubes and 1 white cube.

2. Billy makes a tally mark for each bead he counts.
Which shows how many round beads he counts?

Ⓐ 卌 | Ⓒ ||||

Ⓑ 卌   Ⓓ |

	Total
Round	5
Square	1

3. Look at the graph.

How many fewer bananas 🍌 than oranges 🟠 are there?

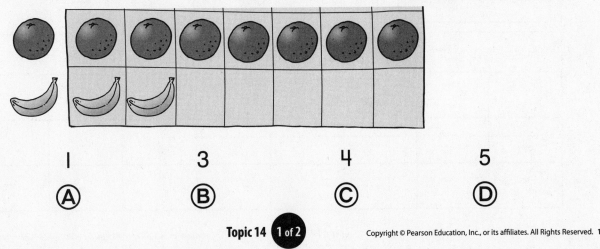

1   3   4   5

Ⓐ   Ⓑ   Ⓒ   Ⓓ

Name _____

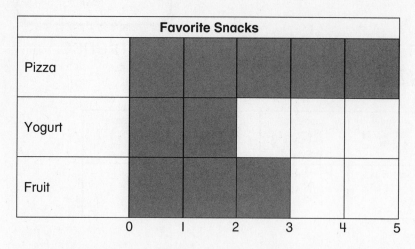

Favorite Snacks

Use the bar graph to answer the questions. Write your answers to questions 4 and 5 on the lines.

Roberta made this graph of her friends' favorite snacks.

4. How many more friends chose Pizza than Yogurt?

_____

5. How many fewer friends chose Yogurt than Fruit?

_____

6. Use the information in the tally chart. Draw pictures to make a picture graph.

Favorite Flower		Tally Marks	Totals
Rose	🌹	|||	3
Daisy	🌼	|||||	6
Tulip	🌷	|||||	5

Favorite Flower						
🌹						
🌼						
🌷						

Name _____

Mark the best answer.

1. Which shape is a triangle?

   Ⓐ ◯

   Ⓑ ▭

   Ⓒ □

   Ⓓ △

2. How many sides does this shape have?

   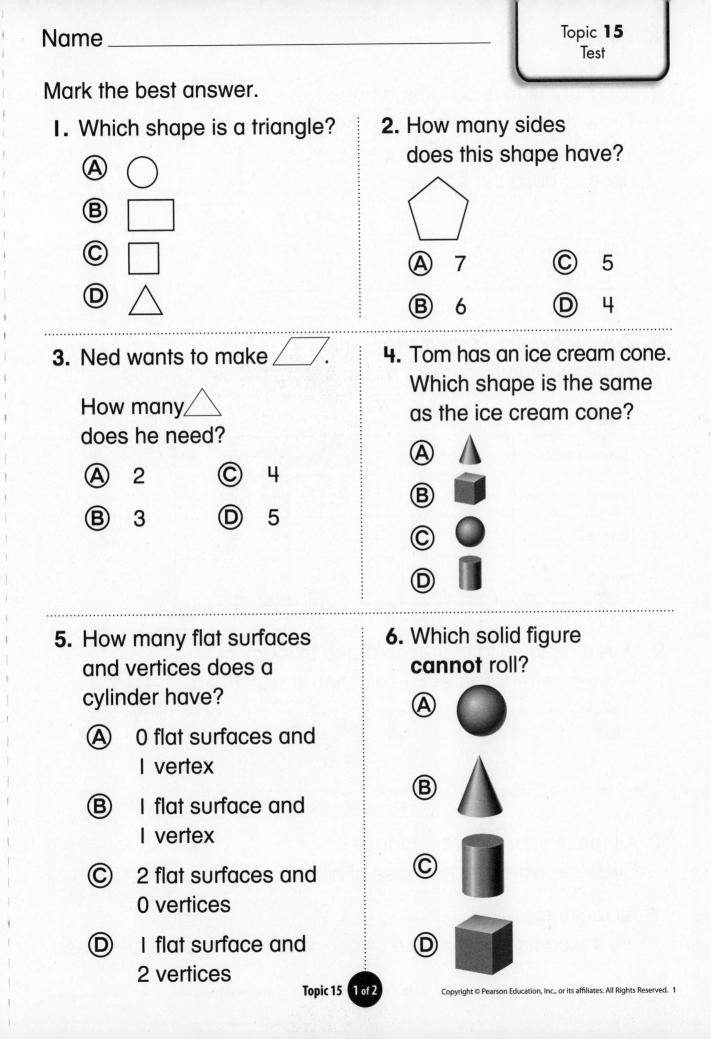

   Ⓐ 7   Ⓒ 5

   Ⓑ 6   Ⓓ 4

3. Ned wants to make ▱.

   How many △ does he need?

   Ⓐ 2   Ⓒ 4

   Ⓑ 3   Ⓓ 5

4. Tom has an ice cream cone. Which shape is the same as the ice cream cone?

   Ⓐ

   Ⓑ

   Ⓒ

   Ⓓ

5. How many flat surfaces and vertices does a cylinder have?

   Ⓐ   0 flat surfaces and 1 vertex

   Ⓑ   1 flat surface and 1 vertex

   Ⓒ   2 flat surfaces and 0 vertices

   Ⓓ   1 flat surface and 2 vertices

6. Which solid figure **cannot** roll?

   Ⓐ

   Ⓑ

   Ⓒ

   Ⓓ

Name _____

7. Mr. Robinson is building a house.
Draw the shape to finish the house.
Write how many of each shape was
used to build the house.

?

☐   ▱   △   ⬡

___   ___   ___   ___

8. Zeke makes an organized list.
Write the number that is missing from his list.

Ways to Make ⬡			
Shapes I Used	▱	⬠	△
Way 1	0	0	6
Way 2	0	2	0
Way 3	_____	0	0

9. Jared used solid figures to make this object.
Write how many of each solid figure was used.

● 🟫 ⬛ ▲

___   ___   ___   ___

10. All these shapes are rectangles.
Circle the words that are true of all rectangles.

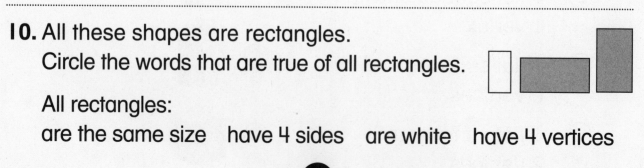

All rectangles:

are the same size   have 4 sides   are white   have 4 vertices

Topic 15 **2 of 2**
Copyright © Pearson Education, Inc., or its affiliates. All Rights Reserved. 1

Name _____

1. Which shape has 4 equal parts?

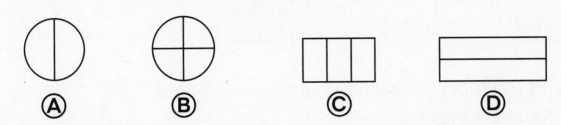

Ⓐ   Ⓑ   Ⓒ   Ⓓ

2. Which shape shows 3 out of 4 equal parts shaded?

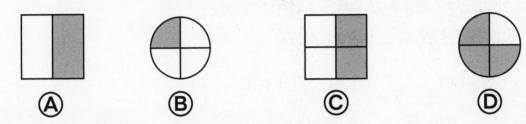

Ⓐ   Ⓑ   Ⓒ   Ⓓ

3. How much of the loaf is shaded?

Ⓐ   1 out of 2 parts

Ⓑ   2 out of 3 parts

Ⓒ   3 out of 4 parts

Ⓓ   4 out of 4 parts

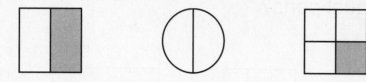

4. Circle the shape where half is shaded gray.

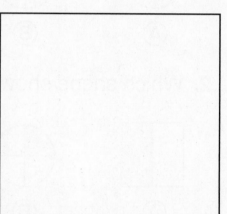

5. Read the story. Draw a picture.
Write the numbers.

Sarah made a scarf with 4 parts.
She made 3 parts red and 1 part blue.
What part of the scarf is red?

_____ out of _____ parts are red.

6. Lucas had a quarter of a fruit bar.
Stella had half of a different fruit bar.
The piece Lucas had was larger.
How would Stella's piece be smaller?
Explain.

_____

_____

_____

1. The 8 cats are black
or white. 7 cats are black.
How many cats are white?

- (A) 8
- (B) 7
- (C) 1
- (D) 0

2. R.J. puts 1 counter
in a ten-frame.
How many more counters
does he need to show 10?

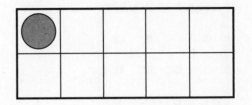

- (A) 10
- (B) 9
- (C) 4
- (D) 1

3. Find the missing part.

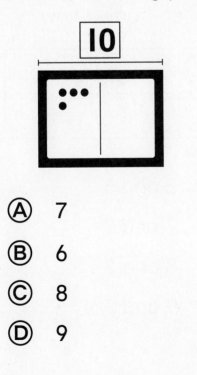

- (A) 7
- (B) 6
- (C) 8
- (D) 9

4. Which subtraction fact can
8 + 3 = 11 help you solve?

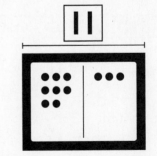

- (A) $11 - 5 = 6$
- (B) $8 - 3 = 5$
- (C) $11 - 8 = 3$
- (D) $3 - 1 = 2$

Name _____

5. Tori sees 8 owls.
5 owls are awake.
The rest are asleep.
How many are asleep?

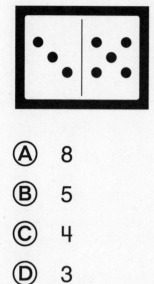

Ⓐ 8

Ⓑ 5

Ⓒ 4

Ⓓ 3

6. 9 children are at the park.
6 children go home.
Which tells about
the story?

Ⓐ 9 − 6

Ⓑ 9 − 3

Ⓒ 9 − 0

Ⓓ 9 + 6

7. Which number sentences
tell about the picture?

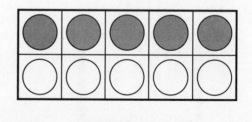

Ⓐ 3 + 7 = 10
7 + 3 = 10

Ⓑ 8 + 4 = 12
4 + 8 = 12

Ⓒ 4 + 7 = 11
7 + 4 = 11

Ⓓ 9 + 3 = 12
3 + 9 = 12

8. Which parts of 10 does
the ten-frame show?

Ⓐ 5 and 5

Ⓑ 7 and 0

Ⓒ 8 and 3

Ⓓ 9 and 2

9. Tina reads 2 poems. Then she reads 5 more. Which shows how many poems in all?

Ⓐ 1 + 5 = 6

Ⓑ 2 + 5 = 7

Ⓒ 3 + 5 = 8

Ⓓ 2 + 7 = 9

10. Ruth has 11 stickers. She gives away 1 sticker. How many stickers does Ruth have now?

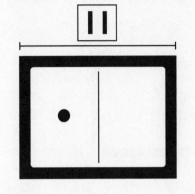

Ⓐ 11 + 1 = 12

Ⓑ 11 + 0 = 11

Ⓒ 11 − 1 = 10

Ⓓ 10 − 1 = 9

11. Which tells about the model?

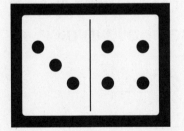

Ⓐ 3 and 4 more is 7.

Ⓑ 3 and 3 more is 6.

Ⓒ 4 and 1 more is 5.

Ⓓ 3 and 0 more is 3.

12. Which number sentence is true?

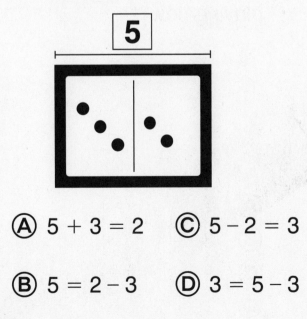

Ⓐ 5 + 3 = 2   Ⓒ 5 − 2 = 3

Ⓑ 5 = 2 − 3   Ⓓ 3 = 5 − 3

13. Micah has 7 plates.
He gives 2 plates to Rosa.
How many plates does
Micah have now?

Ⓐ $7 + 2 = 9$

Ⓑ $9 - 2 = 7$

Ⓒ $7 - 2 = 5$

Ⓓ $5 - 2 = 3$

14. 5 shells are inside the net.
1 shell is outside the net.
How many shells in all?

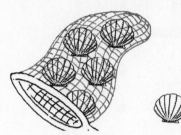

Ⓐ 7

Ⓑ 6

Ⓒ 5

Ⓓ 1

15. 8 monkeys are playing.
1 more joins them. How
many monkeys are
playing now?

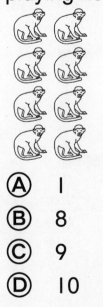

Ⓐ 1

Ⓑ 8

Ⓒ 9

Ⓓ 10

16. April builds 3 birdhouses.
Mark builds the same
number of birdhouses.
How many birdhouses
do they build in all?

Ⓐ $2 + 2 = 4$

Ⓑ $3 + 3 = 6$

Ⓒ $4 + 4 = 8$

Ⓓ $5 + 5 = 10$

Name _____

1. Which number completes the pattern?

10, 20, 30, _____, 50

(A) 30

(B) 40

(C) 50

(D) 60

2. Sarah bakes 5 pies. Joe bakes 7 pies. How many pies do they bake in all?

(A) 57

(B) 17

(C) 14

(D) 12

3. Which number is missing?

___ + 8 = 17

8 + ___ = 17

17 − 8 = ___

17 − ___ = 8

8	9	11	28
(A)	(B)	(C)	(D)

4. Count by 10s to find the number.

(A) 7

(B) 10

(C) 70

(D) 100

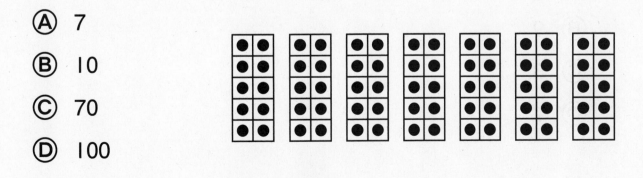

5. 8 toys are in the chest.
6 toys are on the shelf.
Which can you use to
find how many toys in all?

   Ⓐ   8 − 6 = 2

   Ⓑ   6 + 2 = 8

   Ⓒ   8 + 4 = 12

   Ⓓ   10 + 4 = 14

6. There are 20 pens.
10 pens are in each box.
How many boxes in all?

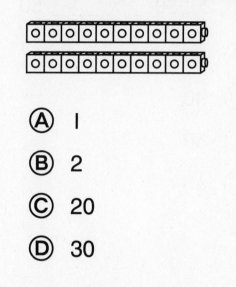

   Ⓐ   1

   Ⓑ   2

   Ⓒ   20

   Ⓓ   30

7. Find the missing
number.

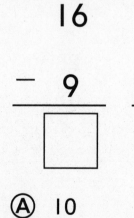

   Ⓐ   10

   Ⓑ   9

   Ⓒ   8

   Ⓓ   7

8. Which number is 10 and
4 ones?

   Ⓐ   14

   Ⓑ   15

   Ⓒ   41

   Ⓓ   13

9. Dallas has 14 stickers and 2 cards. Which doubles fact shows how many stickers per card?

Ⓐ $2 + 2 = 4$

Ⓑ $4 + 4 = 8$

Ⓒ $7 + 7 = 14$

Ⓓ $8 + 8 = 16$

10. Which of these is a way to show 26?

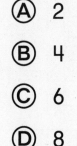

Ⓐ $16 + 26$

Ⓑ $10 + 26$

Ⓒ $10 + 16$

Ⓓ $36 + 0$

11. Annie collects marbles. She has 7 red marbles, 3 blue marbles, and 5 green marbles. How many marbles does Annie have in all?

Ⓐ $7 + 5 + 3 = 15$

Ⓑ $7 + 3 + 3 = 15$

Ⓒ $3 + 5 + 4 = 12$

Ⓓ $5 + 7 + 3 = 16$

12. Count by 2s. How many bugs in all?

Ⓐ 2

Ⓑ 4

Ⓒ 6

Ⓓ 8

  1

Name _____

13. Megan has 6 goldfish, 3 cats, and 1 dog. How many pets does Megan have in all?

Ⓐ $6 + 3 + 9 + 1 = 19$

Ⓑ $6 + 3 + 1 = 10$

Ⓒ $6 + 3 = 9$

Ⓓ $3 + 1 = 4$

14. Which is a related subtraction fact for $7 + 9 = 16$?

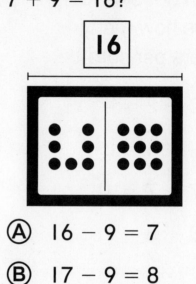

Ⓐ $16 - 9 = 7$

Ⓑ $17 - 9 = 8$

Ⓒ $9 - 7 = 2$

Ⓓ $16 - 8 = 8$

15. Which number is shown?

Ⓐ 22

Ⓑ 12

Ⓒ 20

Ⓓ 23

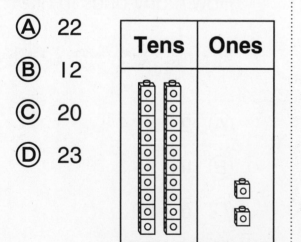

16. Joey buys 15 balloons at the fair. He gives 7 of them to his brother. How many balloons does Joey have left?

Ⓐ $15 - 0 = 15$

Ⓑ $15 - 7 = 8$

Ⓒ $7 - 0 = 7$

Ⓓ $7 - 7 = 0$

1. Leo has 43 stuffed animals. He gives 10 to his cousin. How many stuffed animals does Leo have now?

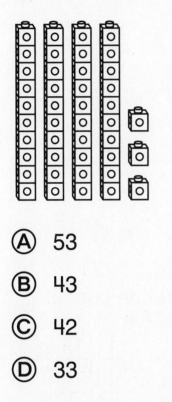

Ⓐ 53

Ⓑ 43

Ⓒ 42

Ⓓ 33

2. Which string is the longest?

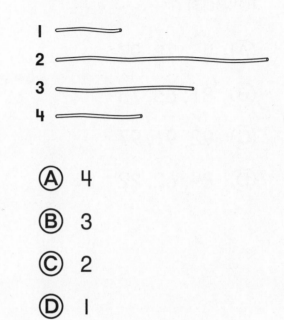

Ⓐ 4

Ⓑ 3

Ⓒ 2

Ⓓ 1

3. George has 27 stamps.
He uses 10 stamps.
How many stamps does he have left?
Which number sentence can you use to solve the problem?
Draw a picture to help solve.

Ⓐ 27 − 10 = 17   Ⓑ 27 − 20 = 7

Ⓒ 17 − 10 = 7   Ⓓ 20 − 10 = 10

Name _____

4. Which shows the numbers in order from greatest to least?

Ⓐ 45, 78, 97

Ⓑ 81, 65, 75

Ⓒ 92, 91, 97

Ⓓ 84, 62, 22

5. Subtract using mental math. Use models if you need to.

88 − 30 = _____

Ⓐ 55

Ⓑ 33

Ⓒ 58

Ⓓ 48

6. Logan's book is taller than Aidan's book. Jack's book is shorter than Aidan's book. Who has the tallest book?

Ⓐ The books are the same height.

Ⓑ Aidan

Ⓒ Jack

Ⓓ Logan

7. Compare the cubes.

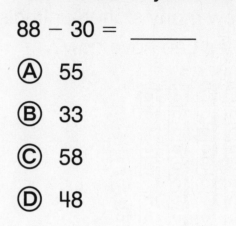

23 ◯ 35

Ⓐ >

Ⓑ <

Ⓒ +

Ⓓ =

Name _____

8. I am a number less than 77. Which number could I be?

- (A) 79
- (B) 78
- (C) 77
- (D) 68

9. Add using mental math. Use models if you need to.

42 + 30 = _____

- (A) 45
- (B) 12
- (C) 82
- (D) 72

10. Which is the best estimate for the length of the pencil?

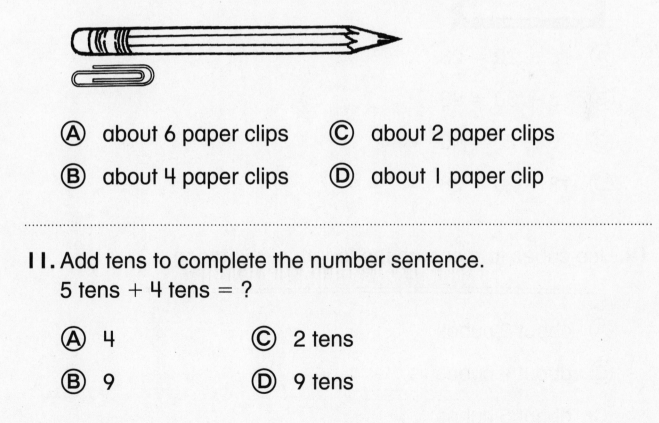

- (A) about 6 paper clips
- (C) about 2 paper clips
- (B) about 4 paper clips
- (D) about 1 paper clip

11. Add tens to complete the number sentence.
5 tens + 4 tens = ?

- (A) 4
- (C) 2 tens
- (B) 9
- (D) 9 tens

Name _____

12. Annie has 18 beads.
Marina gives her 20 more.
How many beads does
she have in all?
Which number sentence
can you use to solve the
problem? Draw a picture
to help solve.

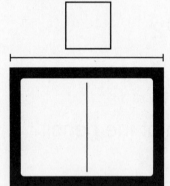

Ⓐ 18 + 20 = 28

Ⓑ 18 + 30 = 48

Ⓒ 20 + 20 = 40

Ⓓ 18 + 20 = 38

13. Subtract tens to complete
the number sentence.
8 tens − 3 tens = ?

Ⓐ 5

Ⓑ 4

Ⓒ 5 tens

Ⓓ 3 tens

14. Use cubes to measure the length of the string.

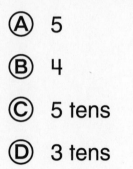

Ⓐ about 2 cubes

Ⓑ about 4 cubes

Ⓒ about 5 cubes

Ⓓ about 6 cubes

Name _____

1. Which time is shown?

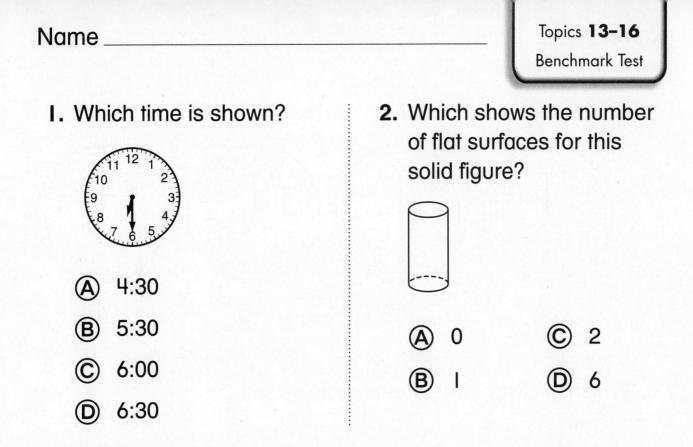

Ⓐ 4:30

Ⓑ 5:30

Ⓒ 6:00

Ⓓ 6:30

2. Which shows the number of flat surfaces for this solid figure?

Ⓐ 0   Ⓒ 2

Ⓑ I   Ⓓ 6

3. Which shape has one fourth shaded?

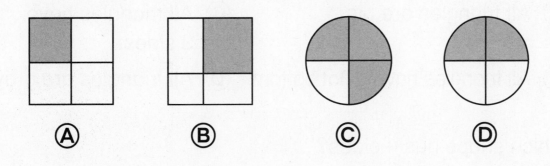

Ⓐ   Ⓑ   Ⓒ   Ⓓ

4. How many more black counters are there than gray counters?

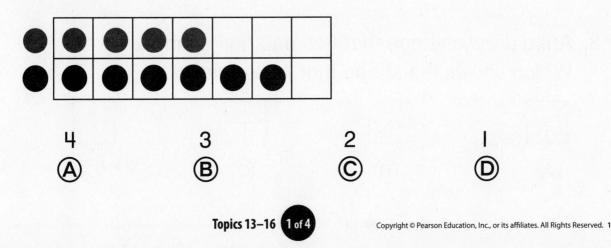

4   3   2   I

Ⓐ   Ⓑ   Ⓒ   Ⓓ

Name _____

5. Which shows 5 o'clock?

Ⓐ   Ⓑ   Ⓒ   Ⓓ

6. Which is always true of a triangle?

Ⓐ All triangles are big.

Ⓑ All triangles have a flat bottom.

Ⓒ All triangles have 3 sides.

Ⓓ All triangles are gray.

7. Which shape has 4 sides?

Ⓐ   Ⓑ   Ⓒ   Ⓓ

8. Anita drew a shape that has one half shaded.
Which shows the shape that Anita drew?

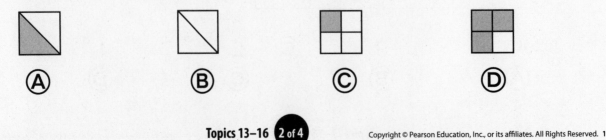

Ⓐ   Ⓑ   Ⓒ   Ⓓ

9. Some children chose their favorite sport. How many fewer children chose Baseball than chose Soccer?

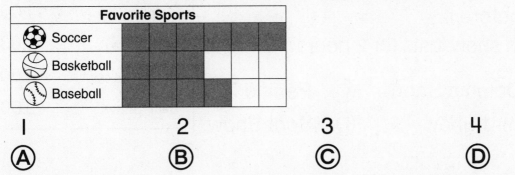

I   2   3   4

Ⓐ   Ⓑ   Ⓒ   Ⓓ

10. Which solid figure is the same shape as this party hat?

Ⓐ Cube

Ⓑ Sphere

Ⓒ Cylinder

Ⓓ Cone

11. Each time Marco spun a color spinner, he made tally marks. How many times did he spin the spinner?

Spinner Colors	
Blue	||||| |||
Red	||
Green	||||| |||

16   17   18   19

Ⓐ   Ⓑ   Ⓒ   Ⓓ

12. Ronny used these 2 solid figures to make an object. Which object did Ronny make?

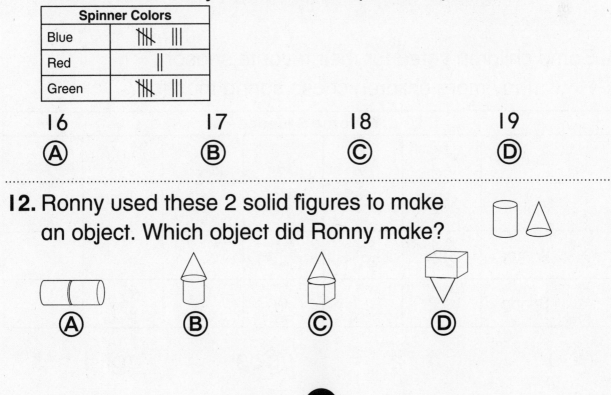

Name _____

13. A zoo has different animal shows. Each show comes right after the one before it.
Which show lasts for 2 hours?

Ⓐ Dolphin Show   Ⓒ Petting Zoo
Ⓑ Bird Show   Ⓓ Seal Show

Animal Show Schedule	
Dolphin Show	11:00
Bird Show	1:00
Petting Zoo	2:00
Seal Show	3:00

14. Max is making a rocket. Which shape does he need to finish it?

Ⓐ ⬡   Ⓒ ▱
Ⓑ △   Ⓓ ▢

15. Which shape shows equal parts?

Ⓐ   Ⓒ
Ⓑ   Ⓓ

16. Some children voted for their favorite season.
How many more children chose spring than fall?

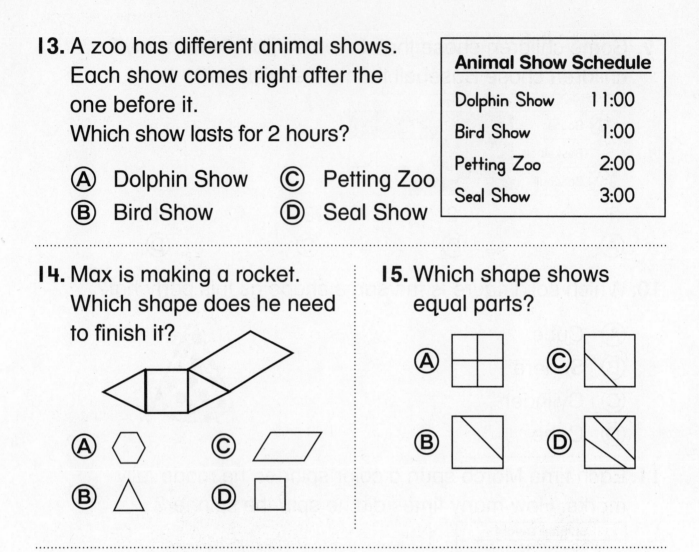

Favorite Seasons

Ⓐ 1   Ⓑ 2   Ⓒ 3   Ⓓ 4

I. Which sentence describes the ten-frame?

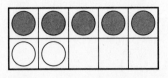

Ⓐ 2 away from 10 is 7.

Ⓑ 5 and 3 is 7.

Ⓒ 4 away from 10 is 7.

Ⓓ 5 and 2 is 7.

2. Which is a related subtraction fact for 8 + 9 = 17?

17

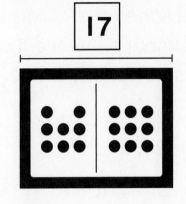

Ⓐ 17 − 9 = 8

Ⓑ 16 − 8 = 8

Ⓒ 9 − 8 = 1

Ⓓ 9 − 9 = 0

3. Each square in this picture shows 10 ones. Which number sentence matches the picture?

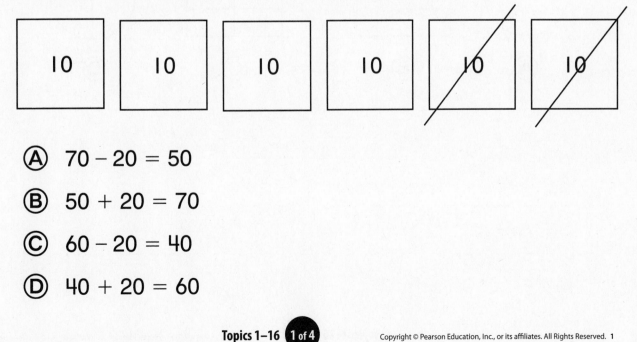

Ⓐ 70 − 20 = 50

Ⓑ 50 + 20 = 70

Ⓒ 60 − 20 = 40

Ⓓ 40 + 20 = 60

4. Diane and Matt have 6 counters in all. Matt has 2 counters. How many does Diane have? Mark the number sentence that shows how many Diane has.

  Ⓐ 2 = 6 + 4

  Ⓑ 6 + 2 = 4

  Ⓒ 4 = 2 + 6

  Ⓓ 6 = 2 + 4

5. Which shows the same time as the clock face?

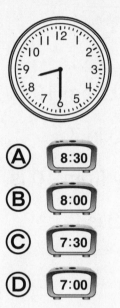

  Ⓐ 8:30

  Ⓑ 8:00

  Ⓒ 7:30

  Ⓓ 7:00

6. Shola sees a rectangle that is divided into fourths. Which is the shape that Shola sees?

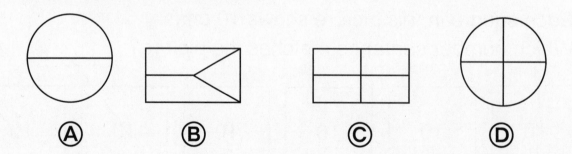

  Ⓐ   Ⓑ   Ⓒ   Ⓓ

Name _____

7. Use this part of the hundred chart.

Skip count by 2s.

Which number comes next?

2, 4, 6, 8, 10, 12, ?

1	2	3	4	5	6	7	8	9	10
11	12	13	14	15	16	17	18	19	20

(A) 13

(B) 14

(C) 15

(D) 20

8. Which best describes the ladders?

(A) The black ladder is the shortest.

(B) The white ladder is the shortest.

(C) The gray ladder and white ladder are the same height.

(D) The gray ladder is the shortest.

9. There are 5 children at the park.
Then 4 more children join them.
Later, 2 more children join them.
How many children are there in all?
Which number sentence helps you solve?

(A) $5 - 4 = 1$

(B) $5 + 4 + 2 = 11$

(C) $5 - 2 = 3$

(D) $5 + 4 + 1 = 10$

10. Which shows the numbers in order from greatest to least?

- Ⓐ 69, 42, 57
- Ⓑ 69, 57, 42
- Ⓒ 42, 57, 69
- Ⓓ 42, 69, 57

11. Subtract tens to complete the number sentence.
5 tens − 3 tens = ?

- Ⓐ 2
- Ⓑ 8
- Ⓒ 2 tens
- Ⓓ 8 tens

12. Some children chose their favorite sport. How many more children chose Soccer than Basketball?

Favorite Sports						
Soccer						
Basketball						
Baseball						

- Ⓐ 2
- Ⓑ 3
- Ⓒ 4
- Ⓓ 5

Name _____

Give each answer.

1. 7 + 2 = ___

2. 3 + 1 = ___

3. 1 + 10 = ___

4. 4 + 1 = ___

5. 8 + 2 = ___

6. 5 + 3 = ___

7. 4 + 2 = ___

8. 6 + 0 = ___

9. 3 + 8 = ___

10. 6 + 1 = ___

11. 1 + 2 = ___

12. 4 + 6 = ___

13. 6 + 2 = ___

14. 5 + 4 = ___

15. 4 + 3 = ___

16. 0 + 10 = ___

17. 4 + 4 = ___

18. 5 + 6 = ___

19. 6 + 3 = ___

20. 3 + 3 = ___

21. 2 + 10 = ___

22. 10 + 1 = ___

23. 1 + 9 = ___

24. 2 + 6 = ___

25. 4 + 8 = ___

26. 3 + 7 = ___

Name _____

Give each answer.

1. $7 + 4 =$ ____

2. $5 + 7 =$ ____

3. $2 + 7 =$ ____

4. $10 + 2 =$ ____

5. $8 + 4 =$ ____

6. $6 + 6 =$ ____

7. $1 + 8 =$ ____

8. $5 + 5 =$ ____

9. $2 + 5 =$ ____

10. $4 + 3 =$ ____

11. $5 + 1 =$ ____

12. $9 + 1 =$ ____

13. $7 + 2 =$ ____

14. $0 + 9 =$ ____

15. $4 + 4 =$ ____

16. $3 + 6 =$ ____

17. $9 + 2 =$ ____

18. $7 + 0 =$ ____

19. $2 + 2 =$ ____

20. $5 + 3 =$ ____

21. $2 + 8 =$ ____

22. $6 + 2 =$ ____

23. $4 + 5 =$ ____

24. $6 + 3 =$ ____

25. $0 + 8 =$ ____

26. $1 + 9 =$ ____

Name _____

Give each answer.

1. $4 + 3 =$ ___

2. $5 + 2 =$ ___

3. $0 + 9 =$ ___

4. $2 + 10 =$ ___

5. $6 + 3 =$ ___

6. $4 + 8 =$ ___

7. $5 + 6 =$ ___

8. $10 + 1 =$ ___

9. $2 + 6 =$ ___

10. $3 + 9 =$ ___

11. $8 + 1 =$ ___

12. $9 + 2 =$ ___

13. $2 + 7 =$ ___

14. $3 + 4 =$ ___

15. $5 + 4 =$ ___

16. $6 + 5 =$ ___

17. $3 + 5 =$ ___

18. $9 + 1 =$ ___

19. $5 + 5 =$ ___

20. $6 + 2 =$ ___

21. $5 + 7 =$ ___

22. $4 + 1 =$ ___

23. $10 + 0 =$ ___

24. $4 + 4 =$ ___

25. $3 + 6 =$ ___

26. $1 + 7 =$ ___

Name _____

Give each answer.

1. $10 - 2 =$ ___

2. $12 - 3 =$ ___

3. $9 - 2 =$ ___

4. $11 - 1 =$ ___

5. $7 - 3 =$ ___

6. $9 - 3 =$ ___

7. $6 - 2 =$ ___

8. $10 - 0 =$ ___

9. $12 - 2 =$ ___

10. $9 - 1 =$ ___

11. $11 - 3 =$ ___

12. $12 - 7 =$ ___

13. $9 - 8 =$ ___

14. $12 - 4 =$ ___

15. $10 - 10 =$ ___

16. $11 - 5 =$ ___

17. $7 - 1 =$ ___

18. $10 - 4 =$ ___

19. $8 - 6 =$ ___

20. $5 - 1 =$ ___

21. $8 - 1 =$ ___

22. $10 - 6 =$ ___

23. $9 - 5 =$ ___

24. $11 - 4 =$ ___

25. $8 - 7 =$ ___

26. $10 - 1 =$ ___

Name _____

Give each answer.

1. $11 - 5 =$ ___

2. $9 - 2 =$ ___

3. $10 - 4 =$ ___

4. $5 - 0 =$ ___

5. $6 - 2 =$ ___

6. $8 - 1 =$ ___

7. $9 - 3 =$ ___

8. $7 - 1 =$ ___

9. $11 - 2 =$ ___

10. $12 - 8 =$ ___

11. $10 - 3 =$ ___

12. $7 - 3 =$ ___

13. $11 - 1 =$ ___

14. $12 - 10 =$ ___

15. $7 - 2 =$ ___

16. $9 - 5 =$ ___

17. $5 - 4 =$ ___

18. $11 - 10 =$ ___

19. $9 - 1 =$ ___

20. $10 - 9 =$ ___

21. $12 - 6 =$ ___

22. $9 - 0 =$ ___

23. $12 - 2 =$ ___

24. $11 - 4 =$ ___

25. $8 - 2 =$ ___

26. $10 - 1 =$ ___

Name _____

Give each answer.

1. $10 - 5 =$ _____

2. $11 - 2 =$ _____

3. $12 - 4 =$ _____

4. $11 - 5 =$ _____

5. $9 - 3 =$ _____

6. $8 - 4 =$ _____

7. $10 - 2 =$ _____

8. $7 - 5 =$ _____

9. $6 - 2 =$ _____

10. $11 - 3 =$ _____

11. $6 - 4 =$ _____

12. $12 - 10 =$ _____

13. $10 - 8 =$ _____

14. $7 - 1 =$ _____

15. $11 - 4 =$ _____

16. $9 - 6 =$ _____

17. $5 - 3 =$ _____

18. $9 - 5 =$ _____

19. $8 - 2 =$ _____

20. $6 - 5 =$ _____

21. $4 - 2 =$ _____

22. $8 - 1 =$ _____

23. $5 - 4 =$ _____

24. $10 - 7 =$ _____

25. $9 - 2 =$ _____

26. $7 - 4 =$ _____

Name _____

Give each answer.

1. 5 + 9 = ____

2. 6 + 7 = ____

3. 8 + 9 = ____

4. 10 + 7 = ____

5. 10 + 10 = ____

6. 8 + 7 = ____

7. 8 + 8 = ____

8. 9 + 10 = ____

9. 8 + 4 = ____

10. 6 + 8 = ____

11. 10 + 8 = ____

12. 6 + 9 = ____

13. 10 + 2 = ____

14. 5 + 10 = ____

15. 9 + 3 = ____

16. 3 + 10 = ____

17. 7 + 9 = ____

18. 9 + 4 = ____

19. 7 + 8 = ____

20. 6 + 10 = ____

21. 8 + 3 = ____

22. 5 + 8 = ____

23. 3 + 9 = ____

24. 9 + 6 = ____

25. 9 + 9 = ____

26. 9 + 7 = ____

Name _____

Give each answer.

1. $6 + 10 =$ _____

2. $6 + 7 =$ _____

3. $10 + 5 =$ _____

4. $5 + 7 =$ _____

5. $9 + 6 =$ _____

6. $10 + 7 =$ _____

7. $9 + 9 =$ _____

8. $8 + 9 =$ _____

9. $7 + 8 =$ _____

10. $9 + 10 =$ _____

11. $4 + 10 =$ _____

12. $10 + 9 =$ _____

13. $9 + 8 =$ _____

14. $7 + 10 =$ _____

15. $9 + 5 =$ _____

16. $8 + 2 =$ _____

17. $1 + 9 =$ _____

18. $5 + 10 =$ _____

19. $7 + 9 =$ _____

20. $4 + 9 =$ _____

21. $10 + 6 =$ _____

22. $3 + 9 =$ _____

23. $8 + 4 =$ _____

24. $8 + 8 =$ _____

25. $7 + 7 =$ _____

26. $10 + 10 =$ _____

Name _____

Give each answer.

1. $6 + 9 =$ ____

2. $8 + 10 =$ ____

3. $4 + 7 =$ ____

4. $2 + 9 =$ ____

5. $8 + 5 =$ ____

6. $8 + 8 =$ ____

7. $10 + 5 =$ ____

8. $7 + 10 =$ ____

9. $9 + 8 =$ ____

10. $3 + 10 =$ ____

11. $10 + 0 =$ ____

12. $7 + 8 =$ ____

13. $2 + 10 =$ ____

14. $6 + 10 =$ ____

15. $6 + 6 =$ ____

16. $10 + 1 =$ ____

17. $9 + 9 =$ ____

18. $2 + 10 =$ ____

19. $7 + 7 =$ ____

20. $7 + 6 =$ ____

21. $7 + 9 =$ ____

22. $5 + 7 =$ ____

23. $10 + 10 =$ ____

24. $6 + 8 =$ ____

25. $10 + 9 =$ ____

26. $8 + 9 =$ ____

Give each answer.

1. $11 - 4 =$ ____

2. $10 - 6 =$ ____

3. $17 - 10 =$ ____

4. $14 - 9 =$ ____

5. $15 - 5 =$ ____

6. $20 - 10 =$ ____

7. $13 - 3 =$ ____

8. $12 - 6 =$ ____

9. $16 - 10 =$ ____

10. $11 - 6 =$ ____

11. $15 - 7 =$ ____

12. $18 - 9 =$ ____

13. $19 - 10 =$ ____

14. $17 - 8 =$ ____

15. $14 - 7 =$ ____

16. $10 - 4 =$ ____

17. $18 - 8 =$ ____

18. $12 - 3 =$ ____

19. $14 - 5 =$ ____

20. $13 - 6 =$ ____

21. $19 - 9 =$ ____

22. $15 - 9 =$ ____

23. $12 - 4 =$ ____

24. $16 - 8 =$ ____

25. $13 - 9 =$ ____

26. $15 - 10 =$ ____

Name _____

Give each answer.

1. $10 - 4 =$ ____

2. $16 - 6 =$ ____

3. $12 - 10 =$ ____

4. $11 - 9 =$ ____

5. $14 - 4 =$ ____

6. $15 - 8 =$ ____

7. $13 - 4 =$ ____

8. $20 - 10 =$ ____

9. $18 - 9 =$ ____

10. $17 - 7 =$ ____

11. $12 - 8 =$ ____

12. $18 - 8 =$ ____

13. $13 - 3 =$ ____

14. $19 - 9 =$ ____

15. $11 - 10 =$ ____

16. $16 - 9 =$ ____

17. $12 - 9 =$ ____

18. $14 - 6 =$ ____

19. $14 - 10 =$ ____

20. $18 - 9 =$ ____

21. $19 - 10 =$ ____

22. $14 - 9 =$ ____

23. $11 - 8 =$ ____

24. $13 - 5 =$ ____

25. $12 - 6 =$ ____

26. $15 - 9 =$ ____

Name _____

Give each answer.

1. $15 - 9 =$ ___

2. $18 - 8 =$ ___

3. $12 - 2 =$ ___

4. $11 - 10 =$ ___

5. $15 - 5 =$ ___

6. $16 - 10 =$ ___

7. $18 - 9 =$ ___

8. $17 - 9 =$ ___

9. $16 - 8 =$ ___

10. $14 - 7 =$ ___

11. $20 - 10 =$ ___

12. $12 - 10 =$ ___

13. $15 - 8 =$ ___

14. $12 - 3 =$ ___

15. $18 - 10 =$ ___

16. $16 - 9 =$ ___

17. $14 - 8 =$ ___

18. $19 - 9 =$ ___

19. $13 - 6 =$ ___

20. $14 - 9 =$ ___

21. $16 - 6 =$ ___

22. $13 - 8 =$ ___

23. $12 - 5 =$ ___

24. $15 - 7 =$ ___

25. $16 - 7 =$ ___

26. $15 - 6 =$ ___